Drawing Practice Book

This book belongs to:

_____

© Innate Press

_____

How does it work?

Did you know that artists often use references when they draw? They may go outside and look at a tree in person or use a photograph of something they want to draw. It helps to have something to look at while drawing to get an idea of the scale and details of the object.

In this drawing practice book, each page has a picture for you to use as a reference as you draw. Will your drawings look exactly like the photographs? Of course not! They are there for inspiration and reference. Draw each picture three times to practice your drawing skills. Or, you can try drawing the object in three different styles.

No matter how you use this book, we hope you have fun drawing!

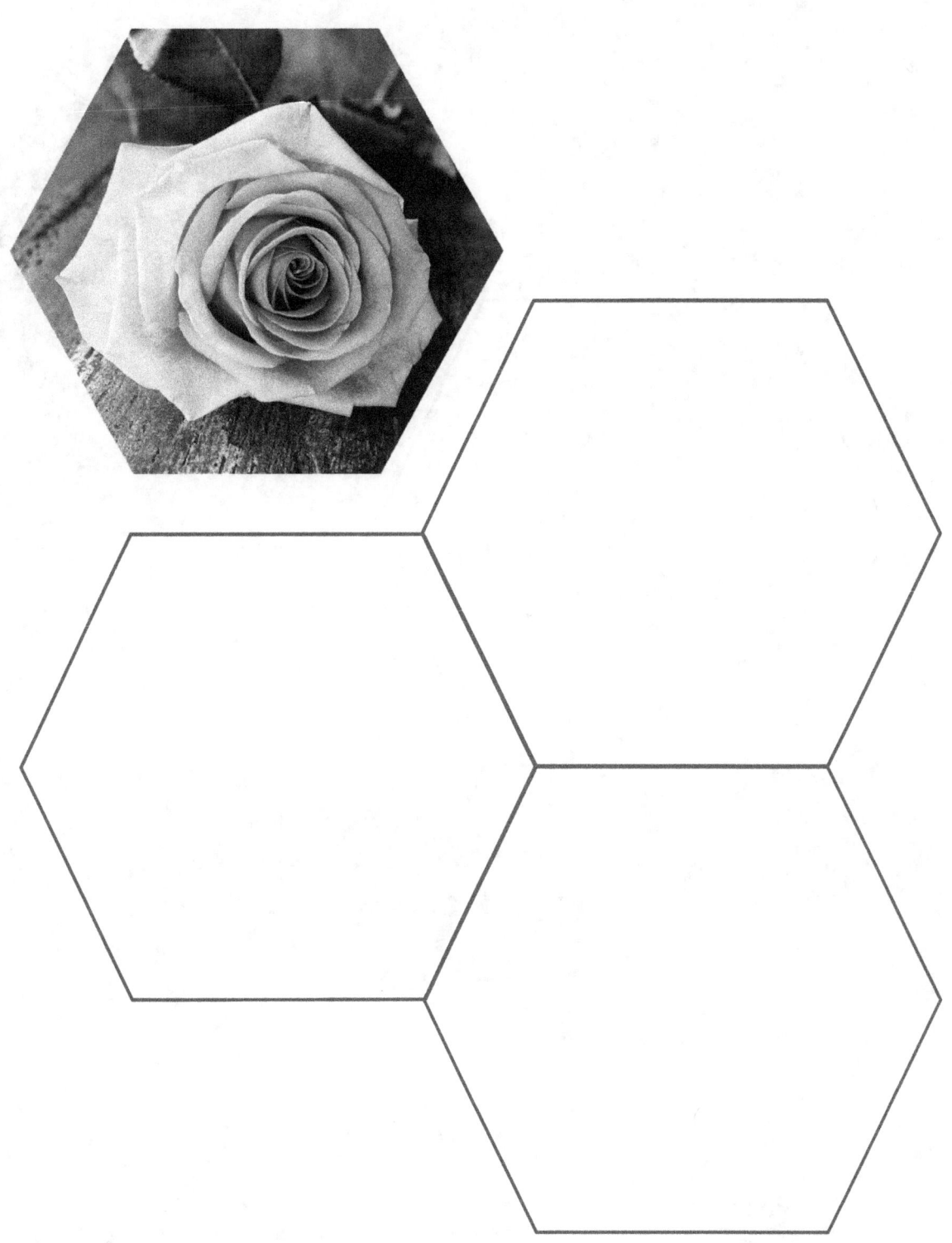

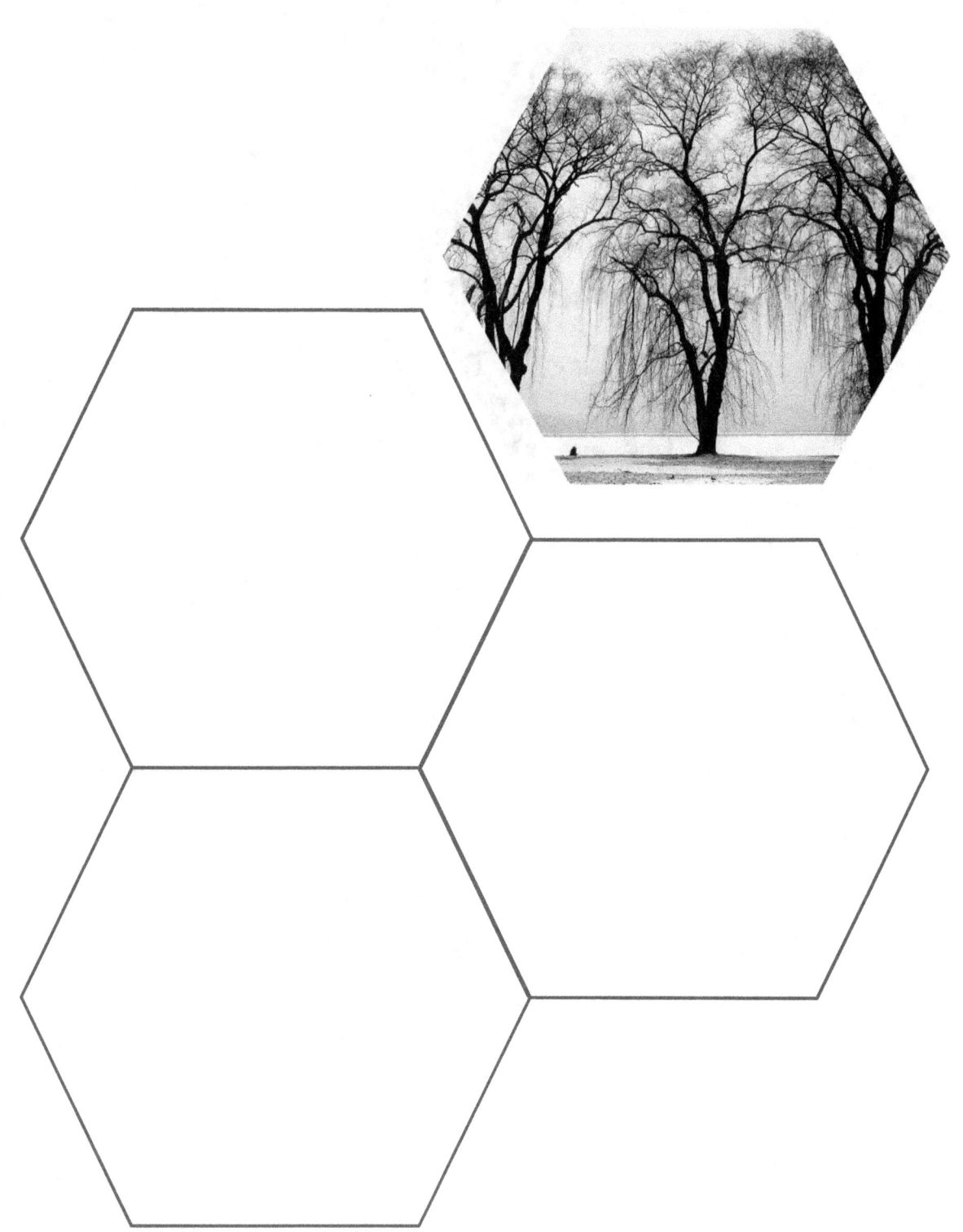

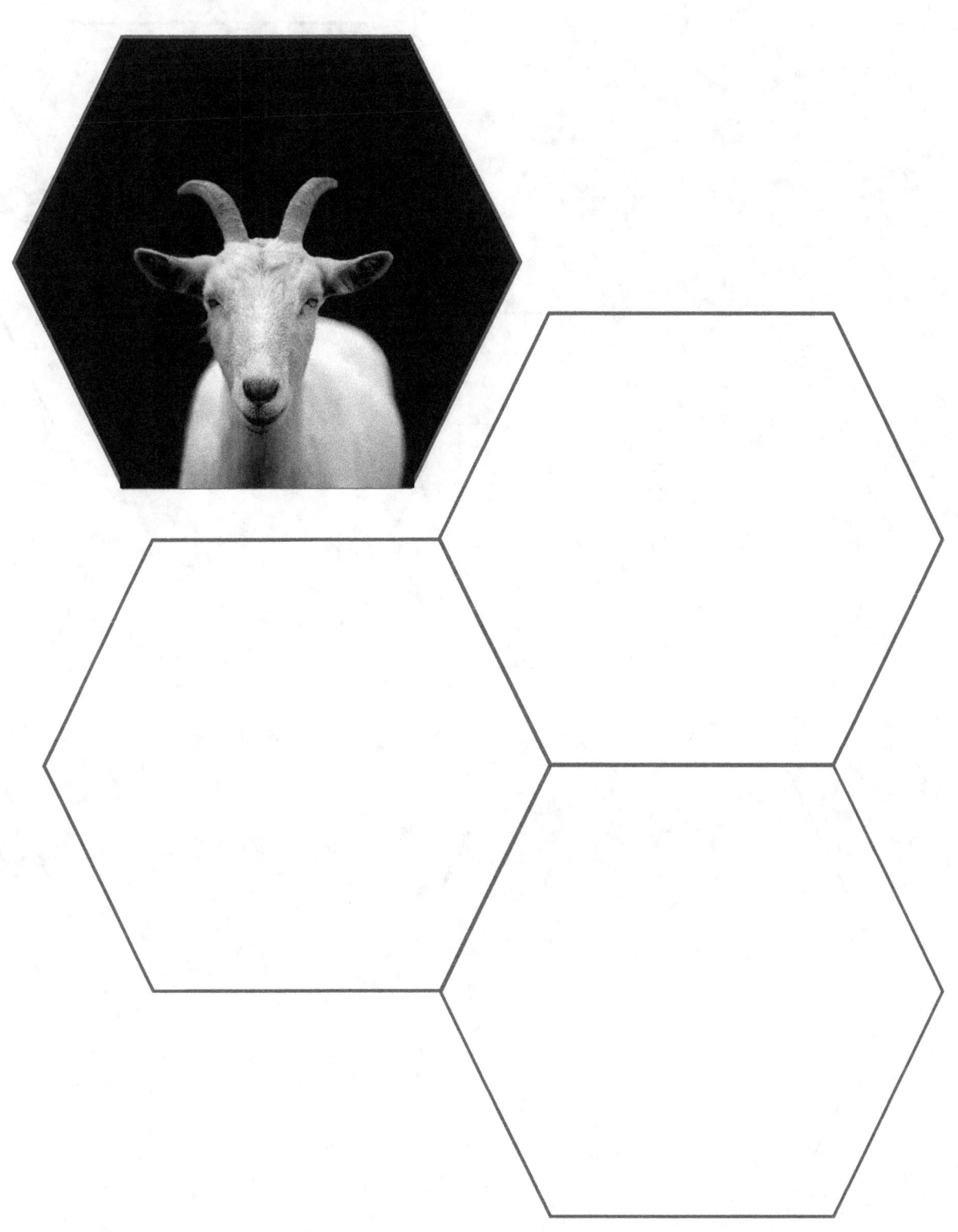

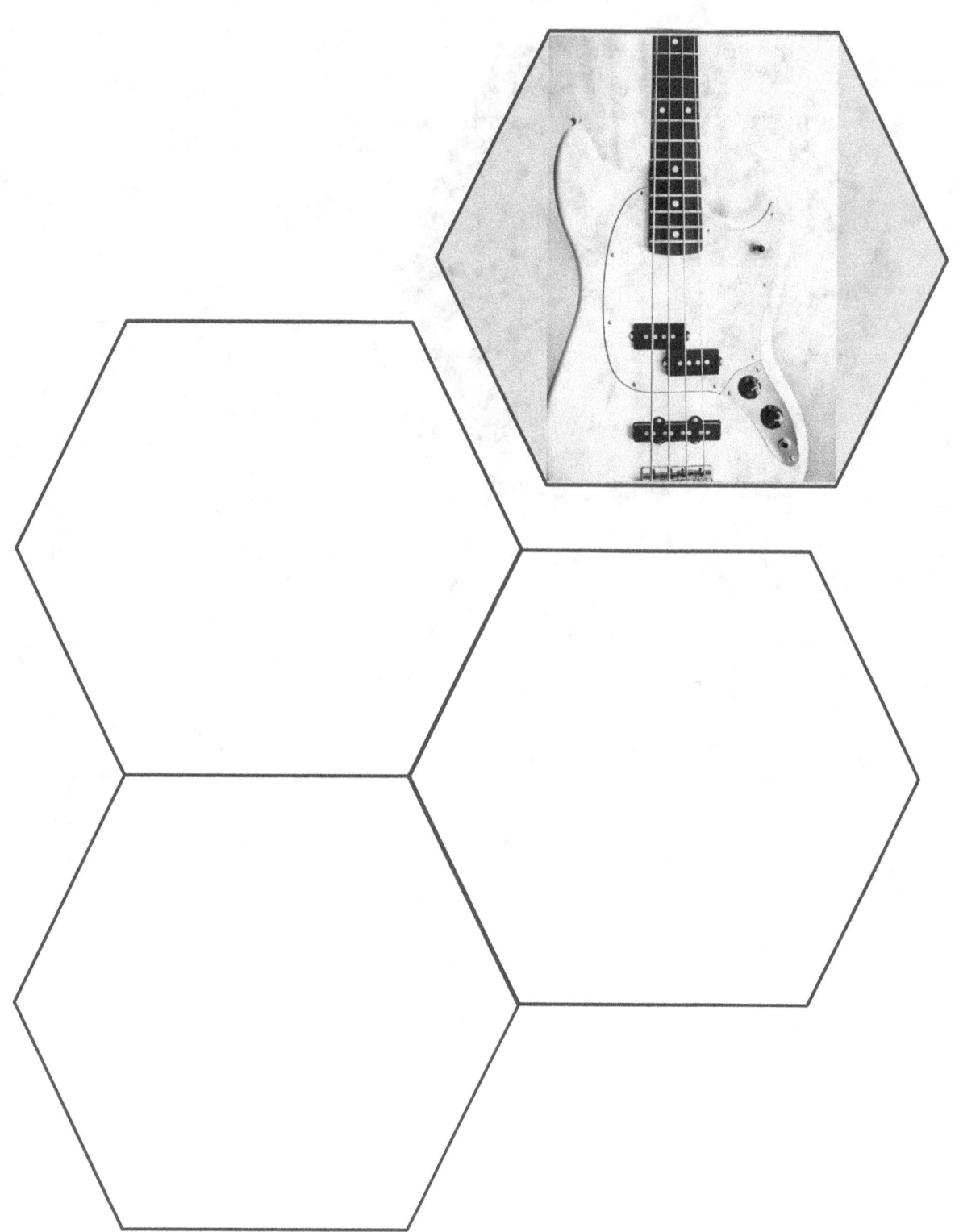

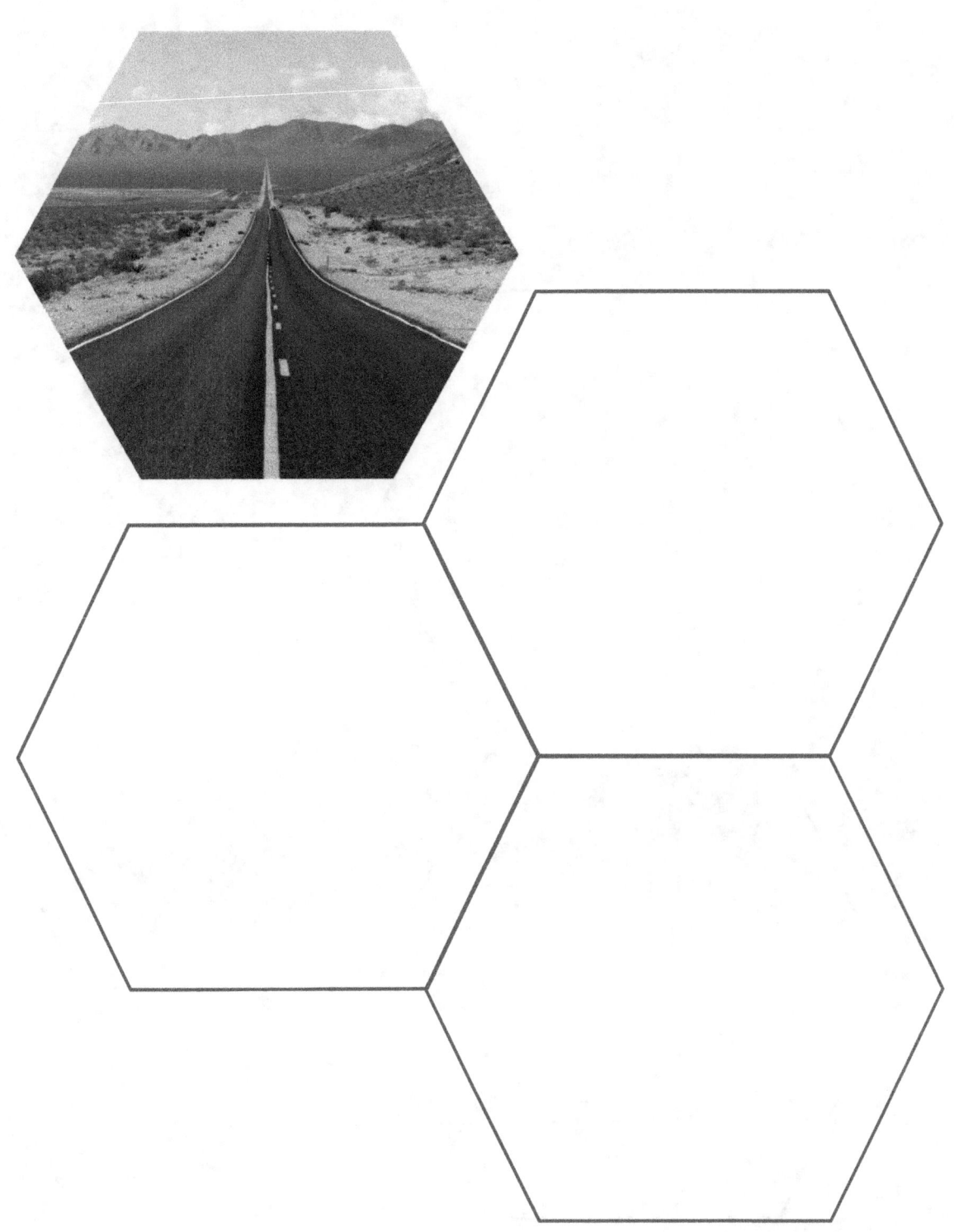

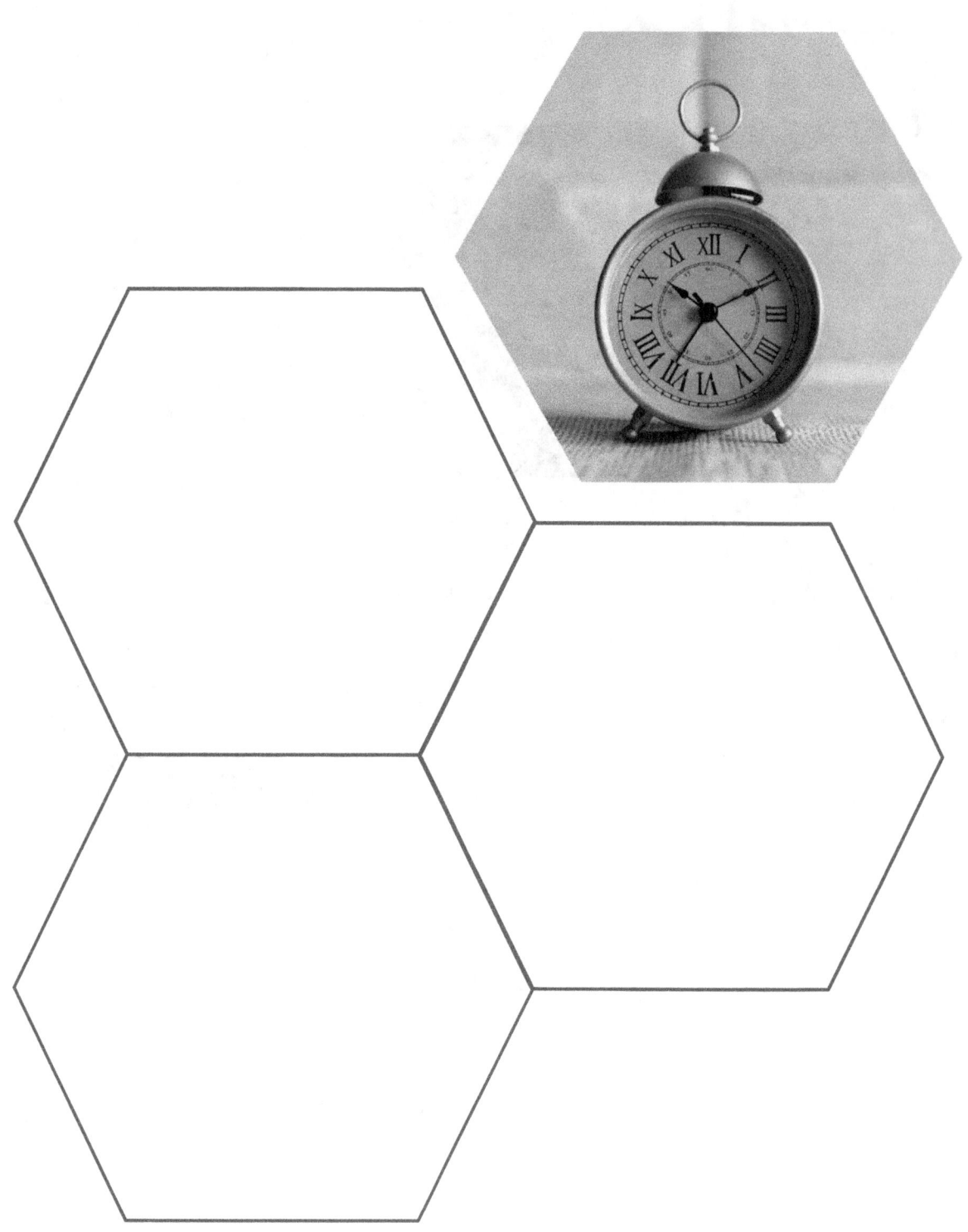

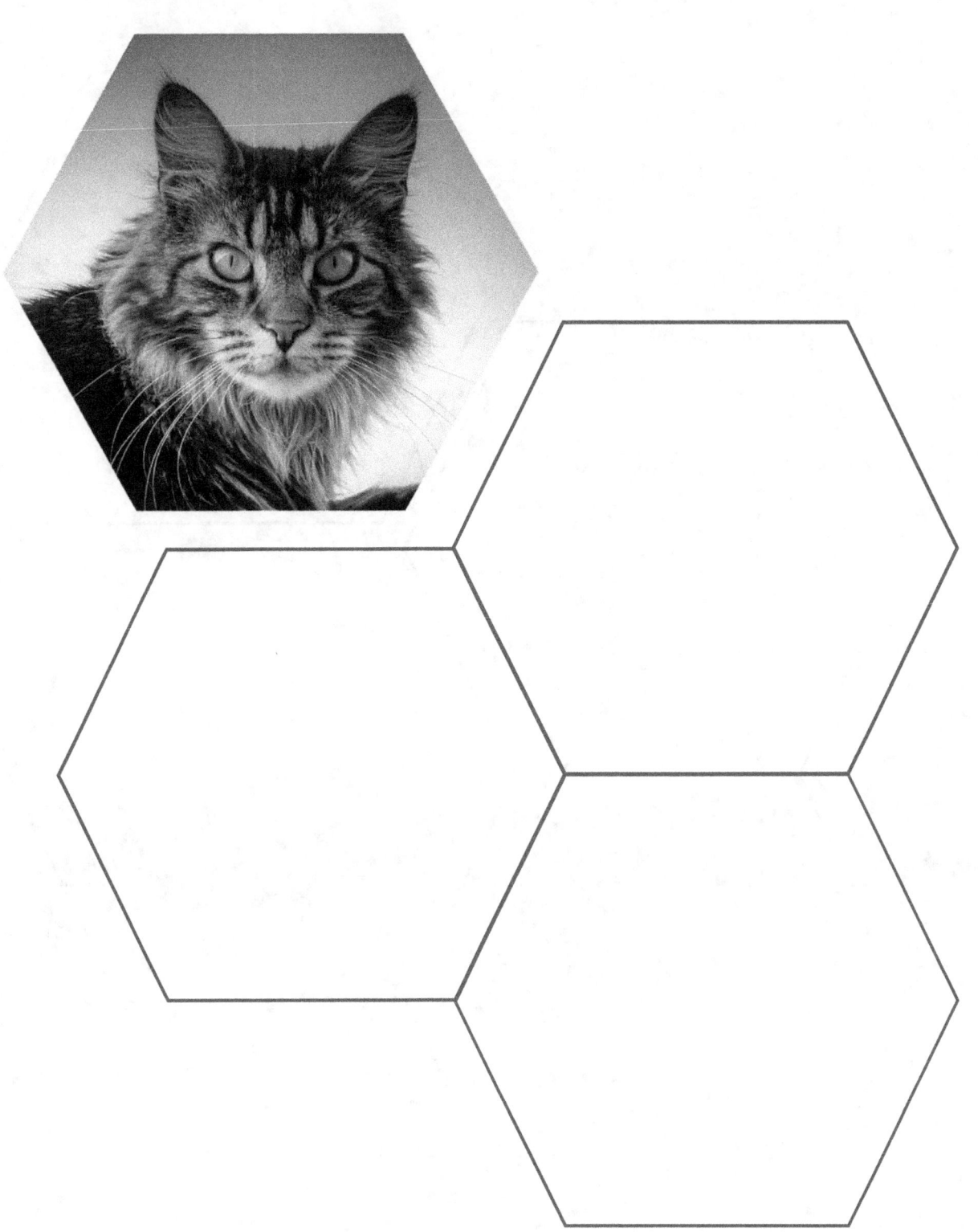

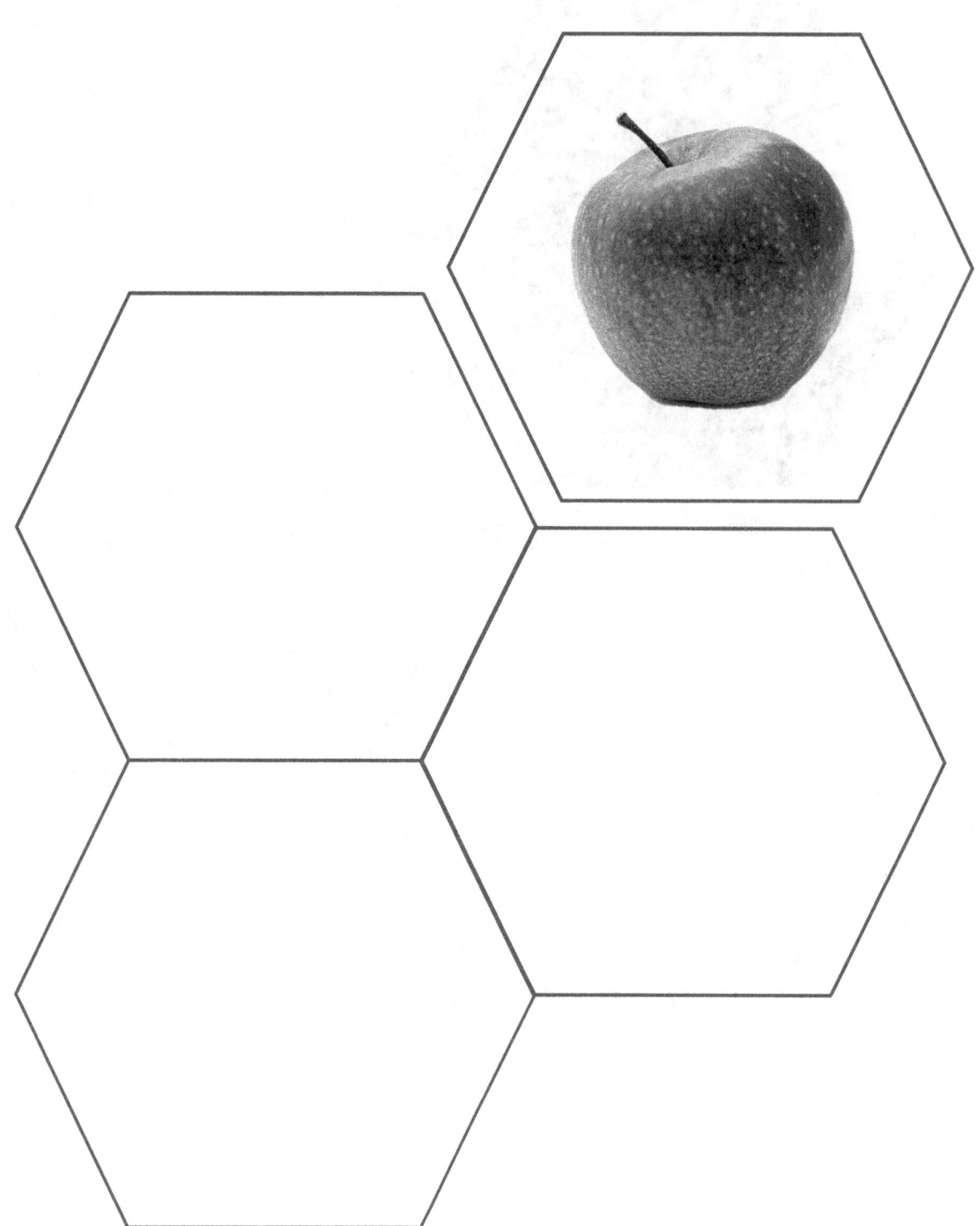

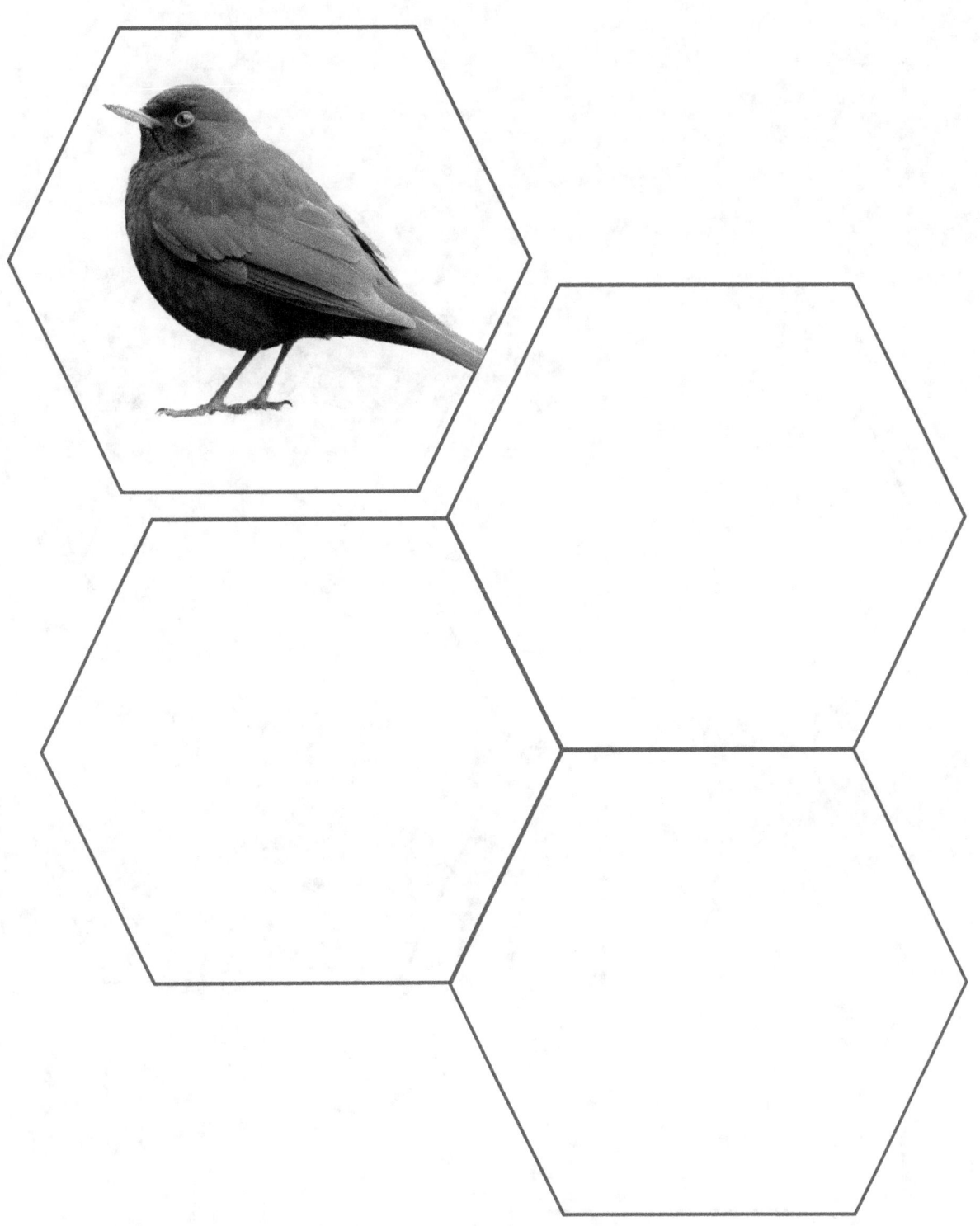

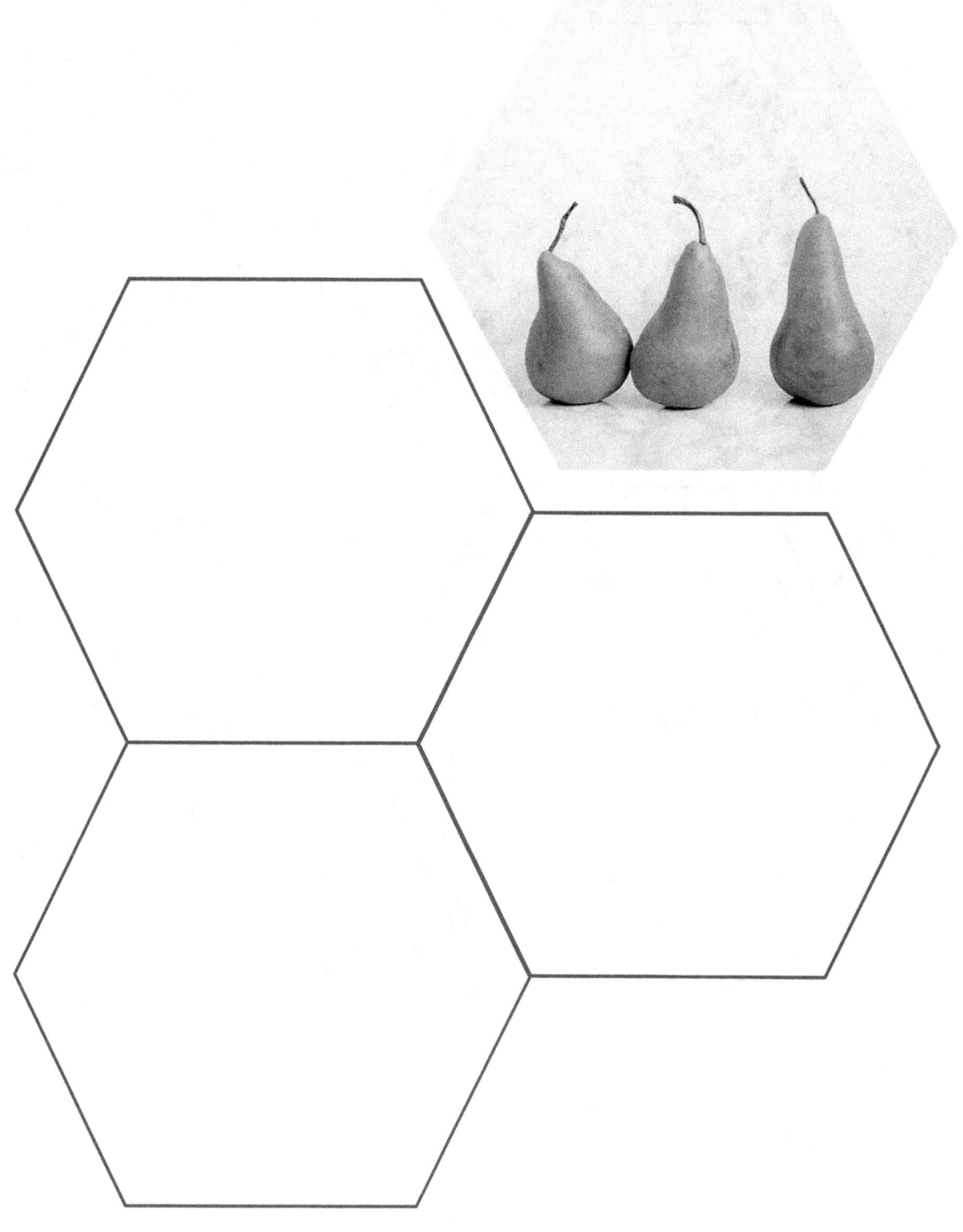

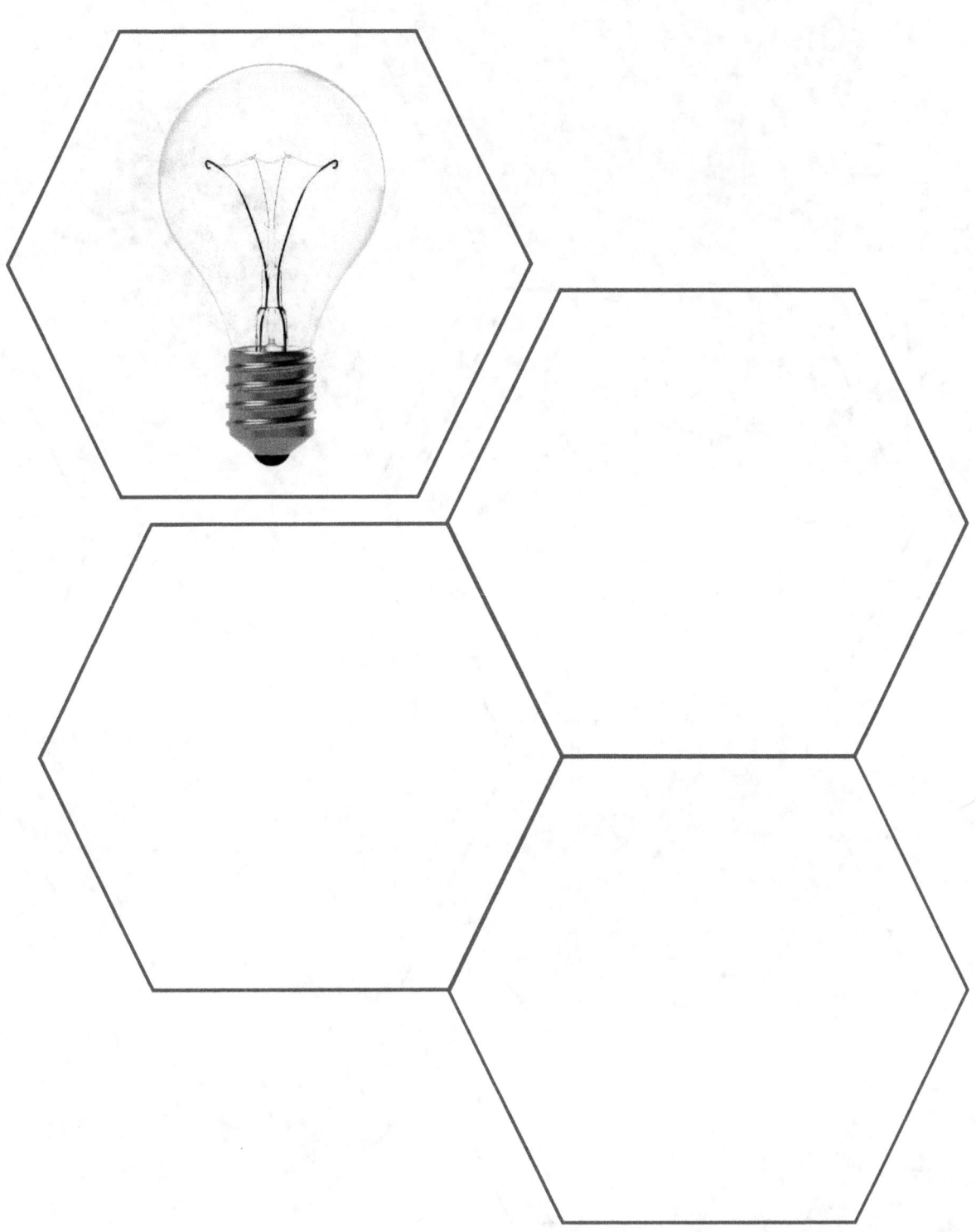

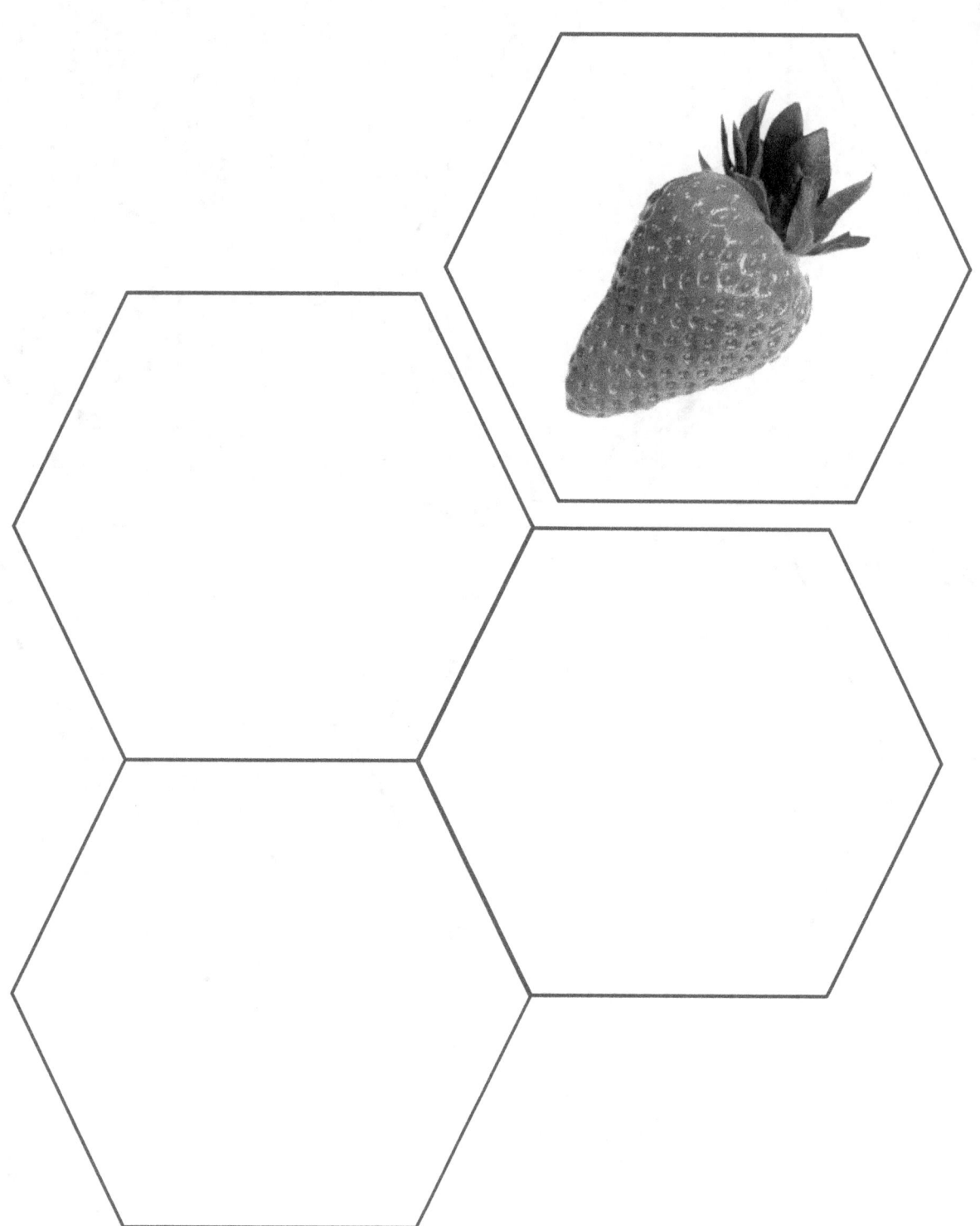

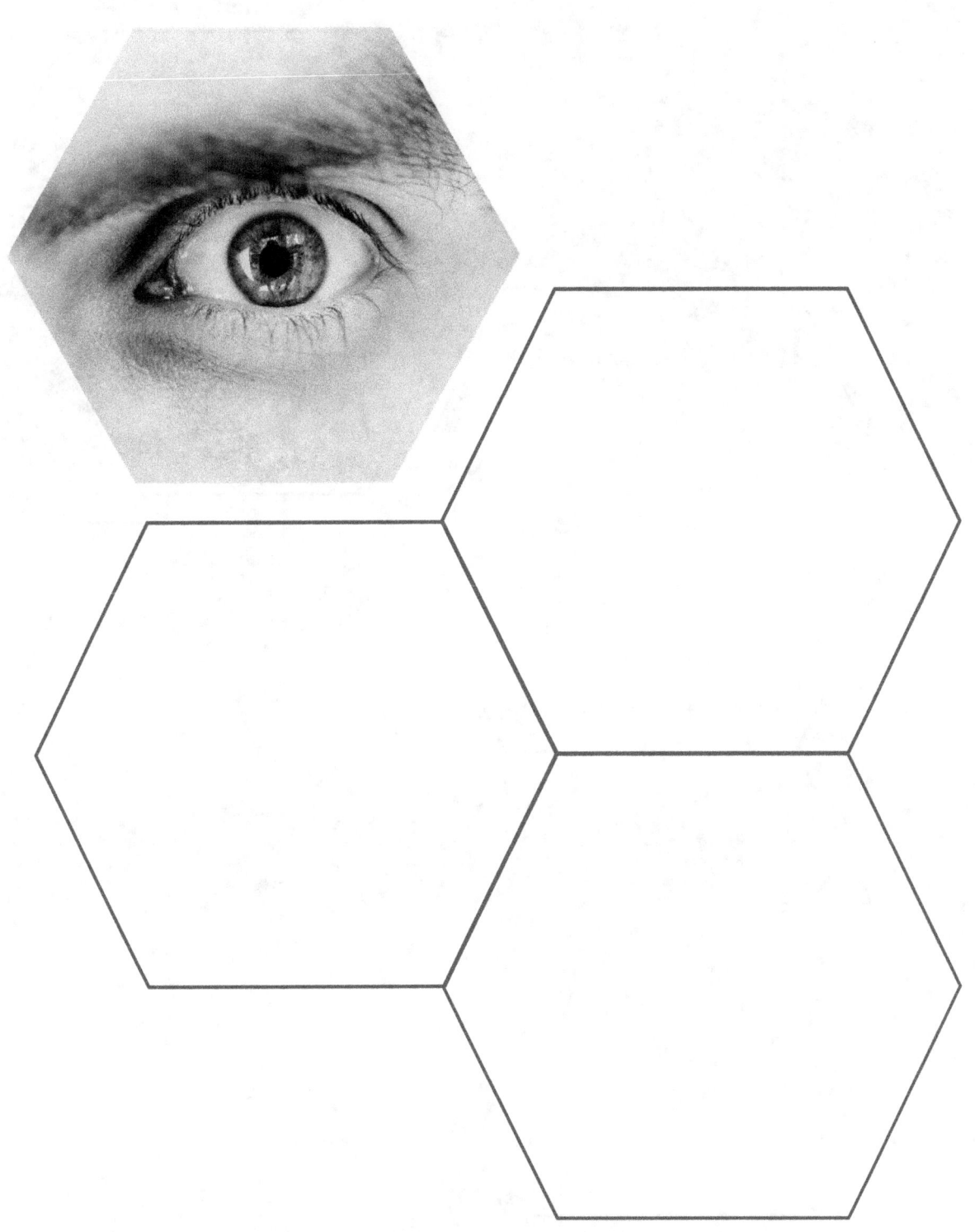

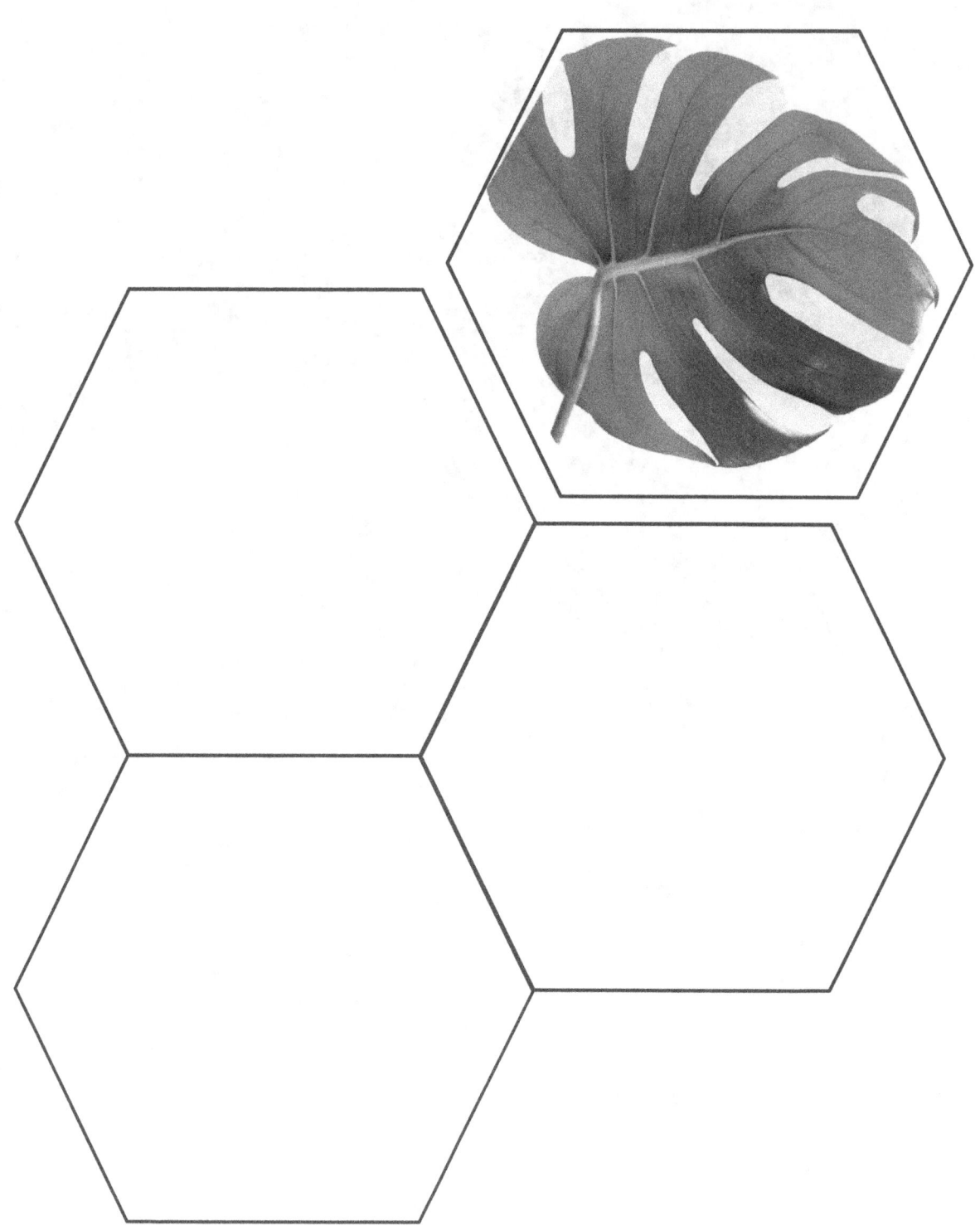

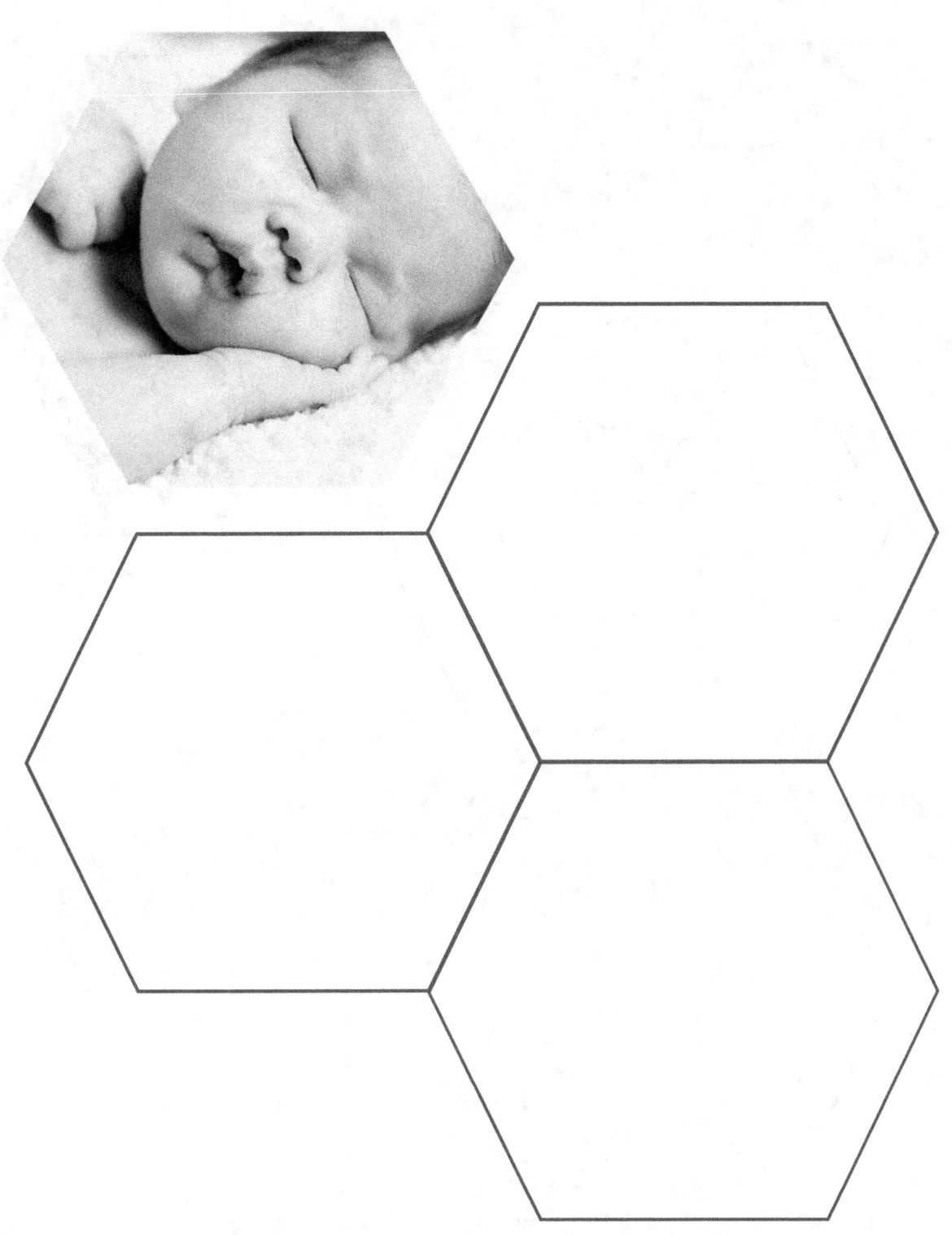

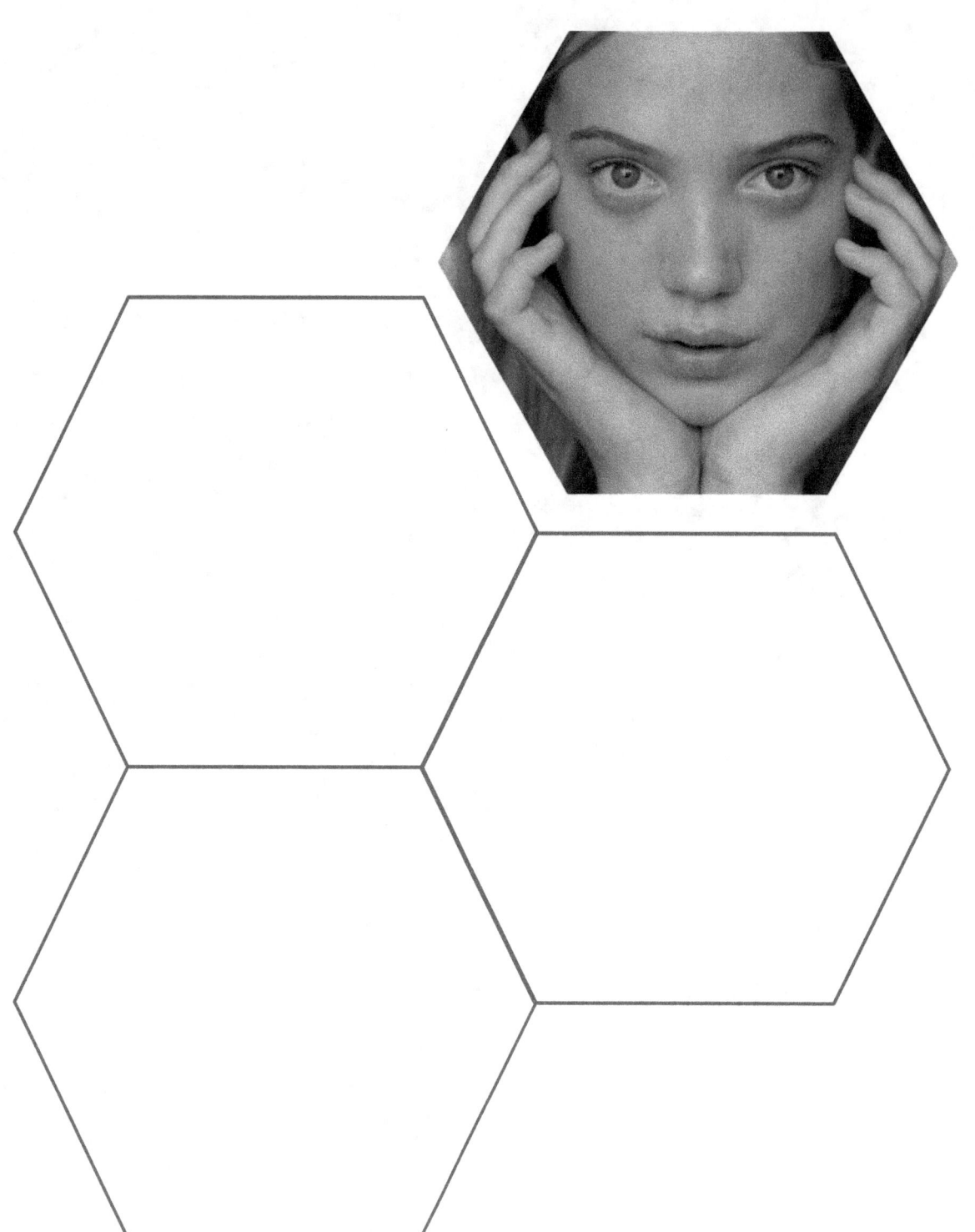

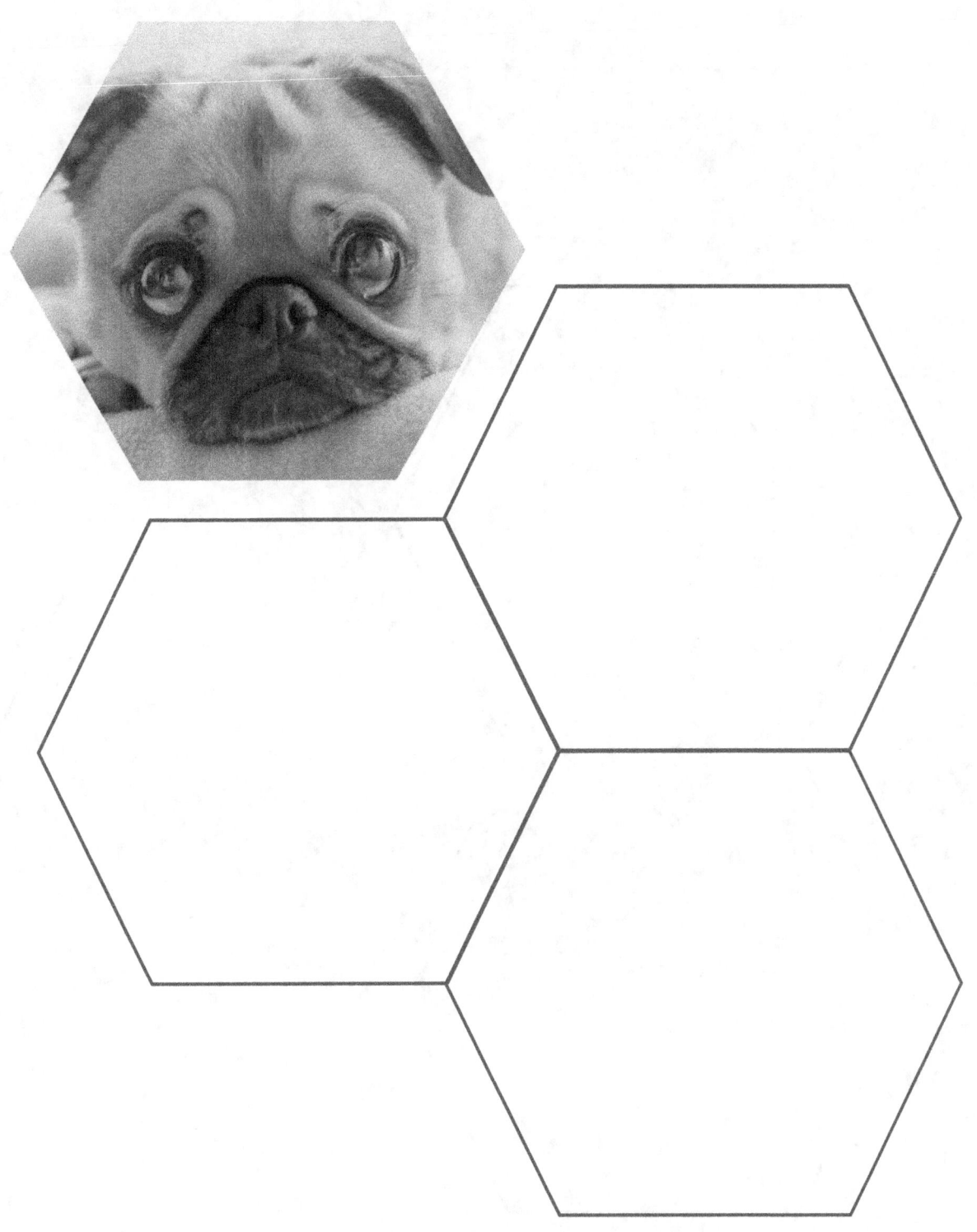

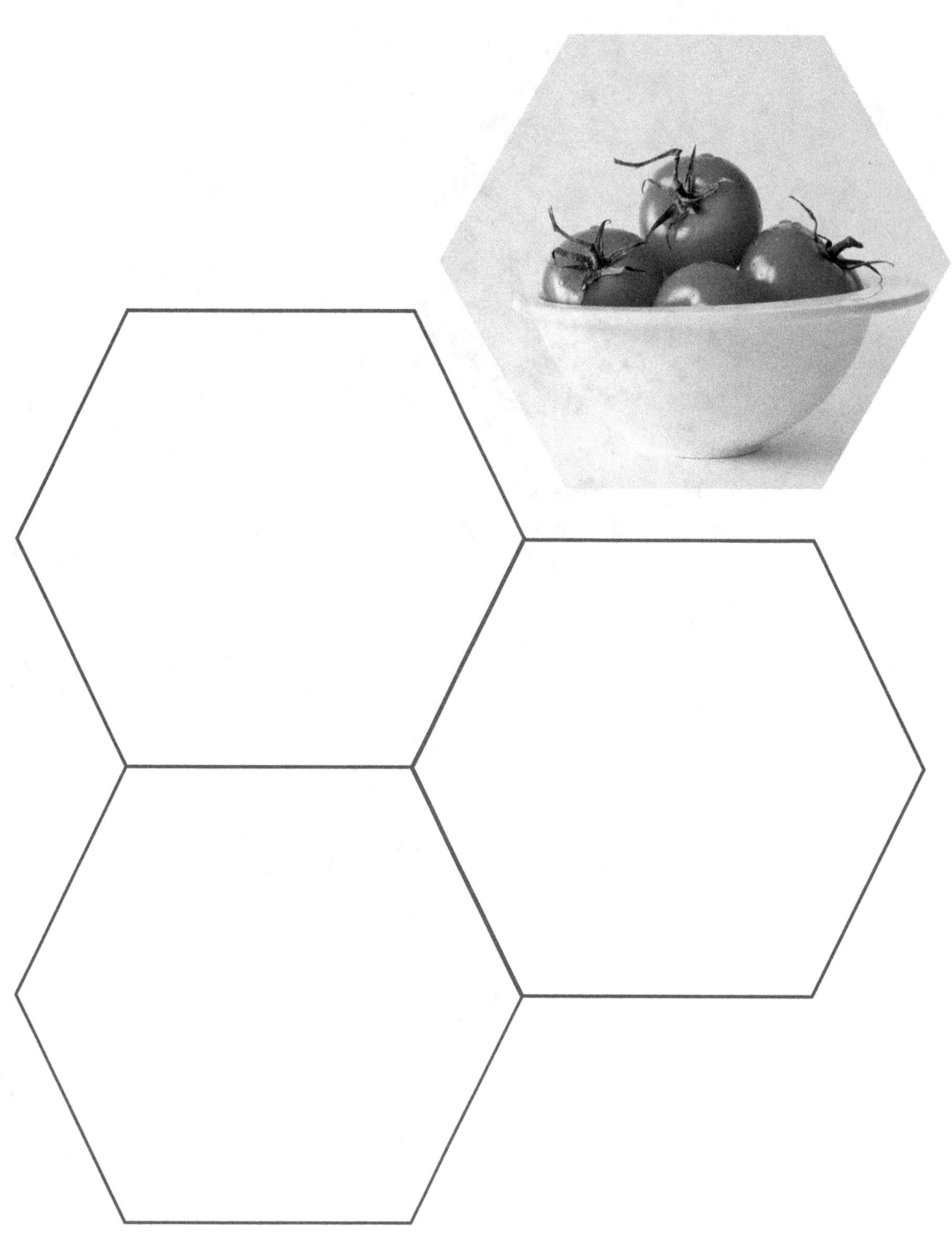

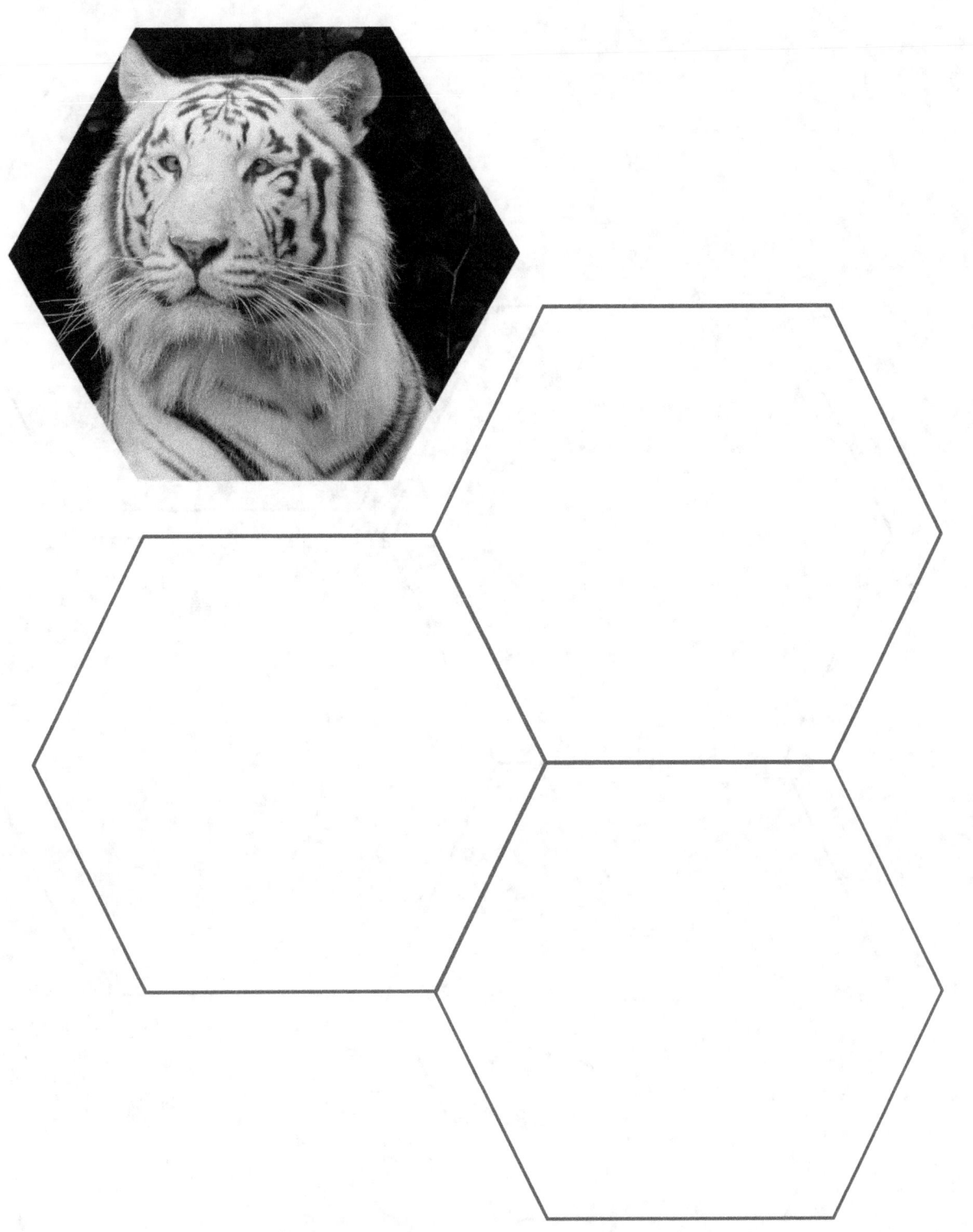

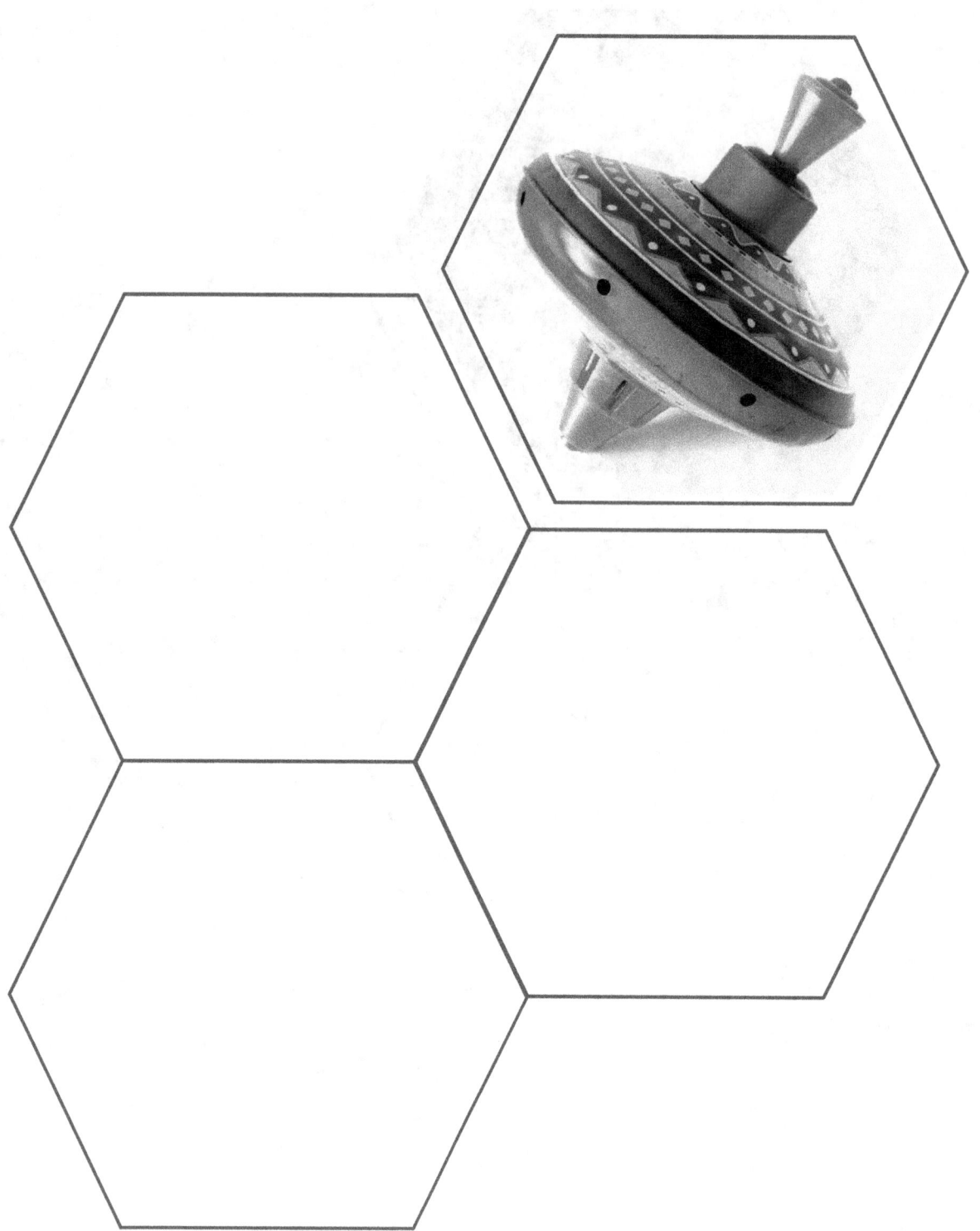

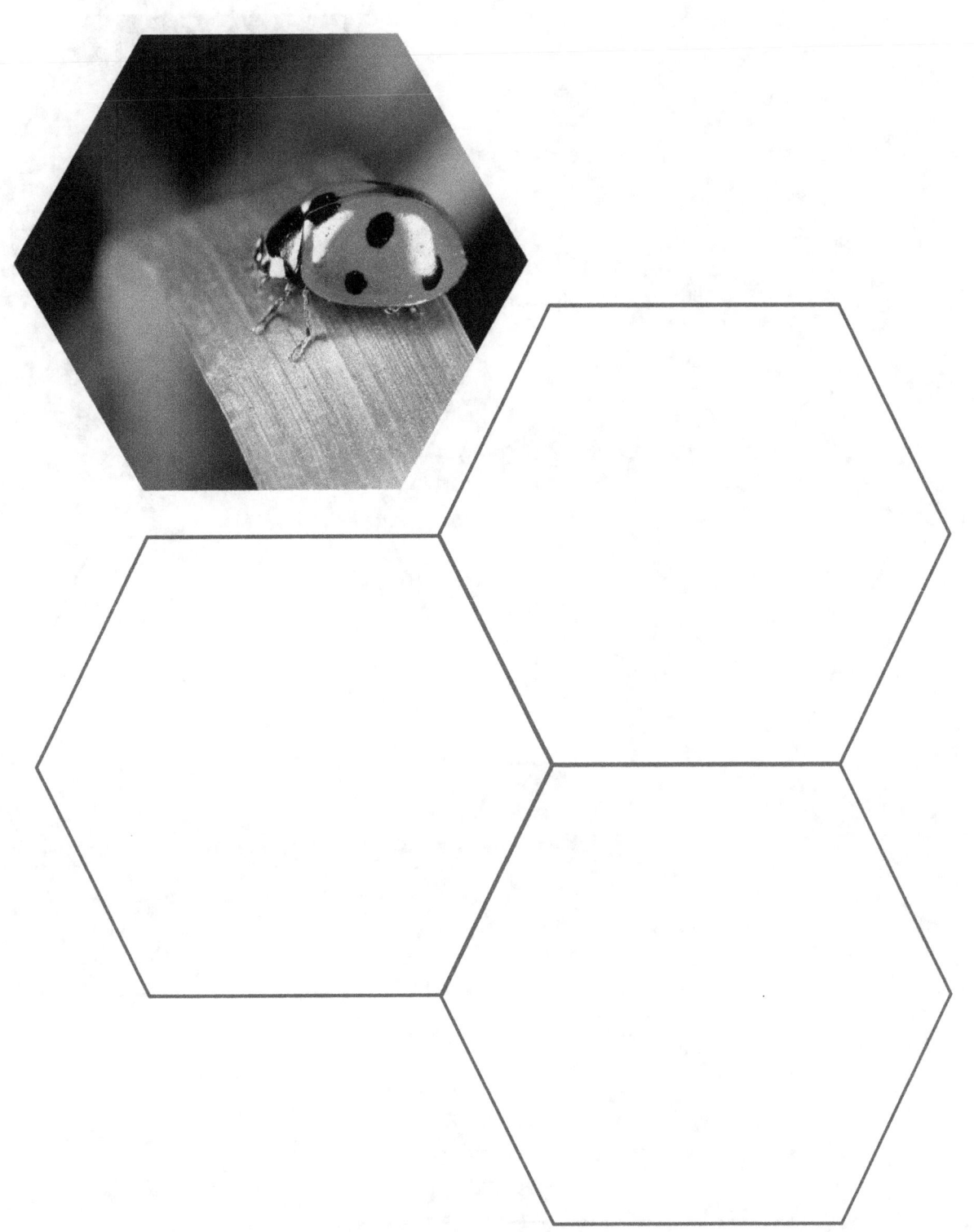

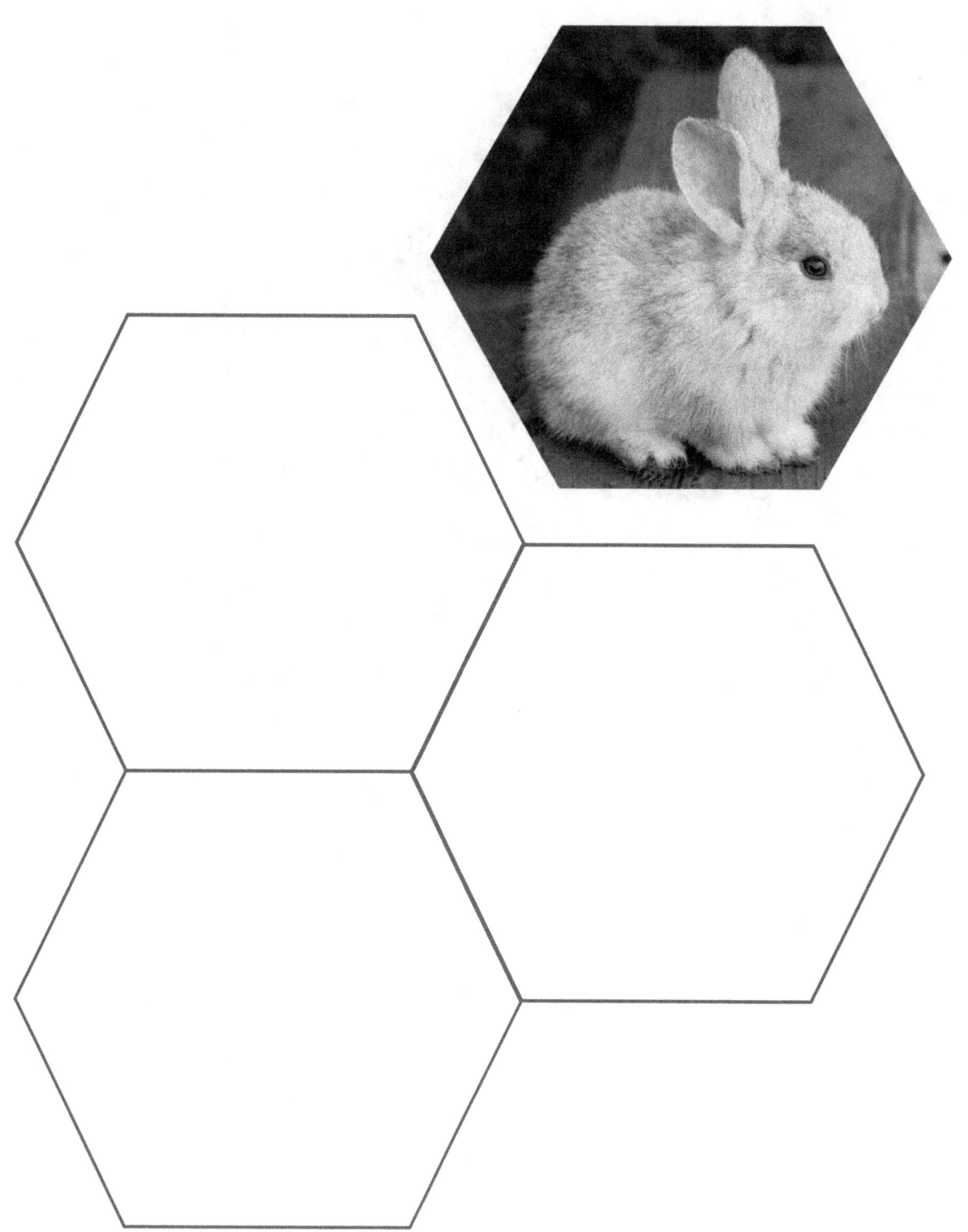

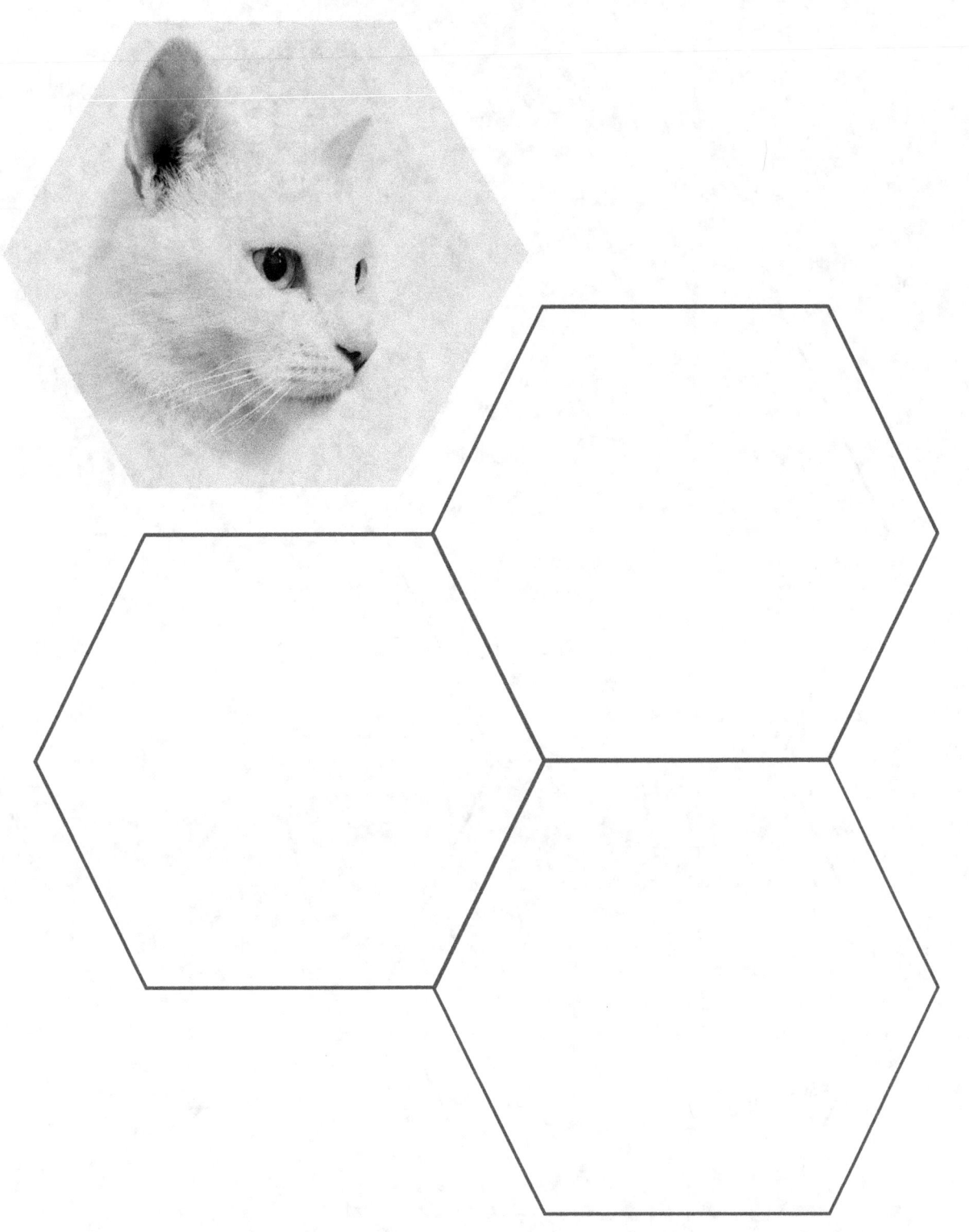

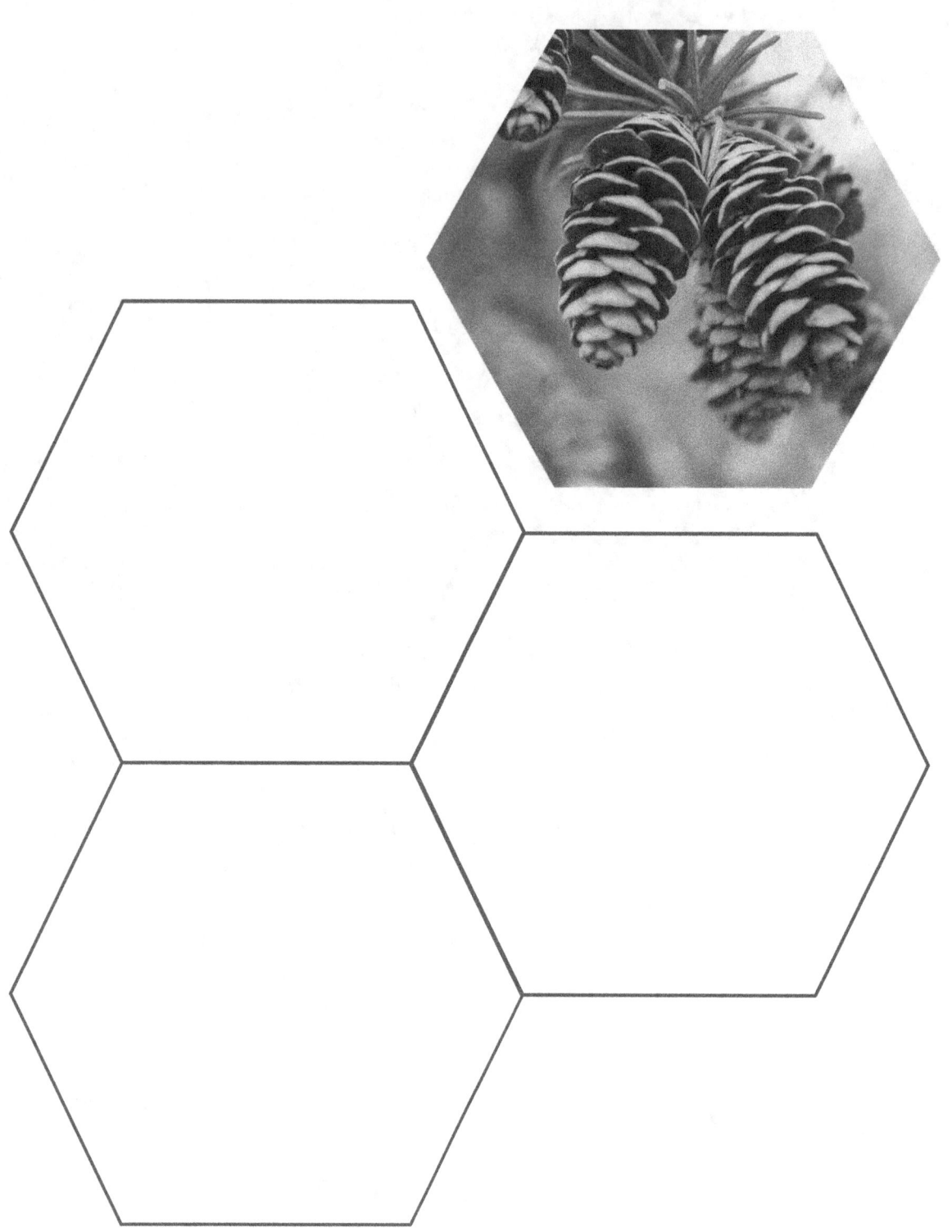

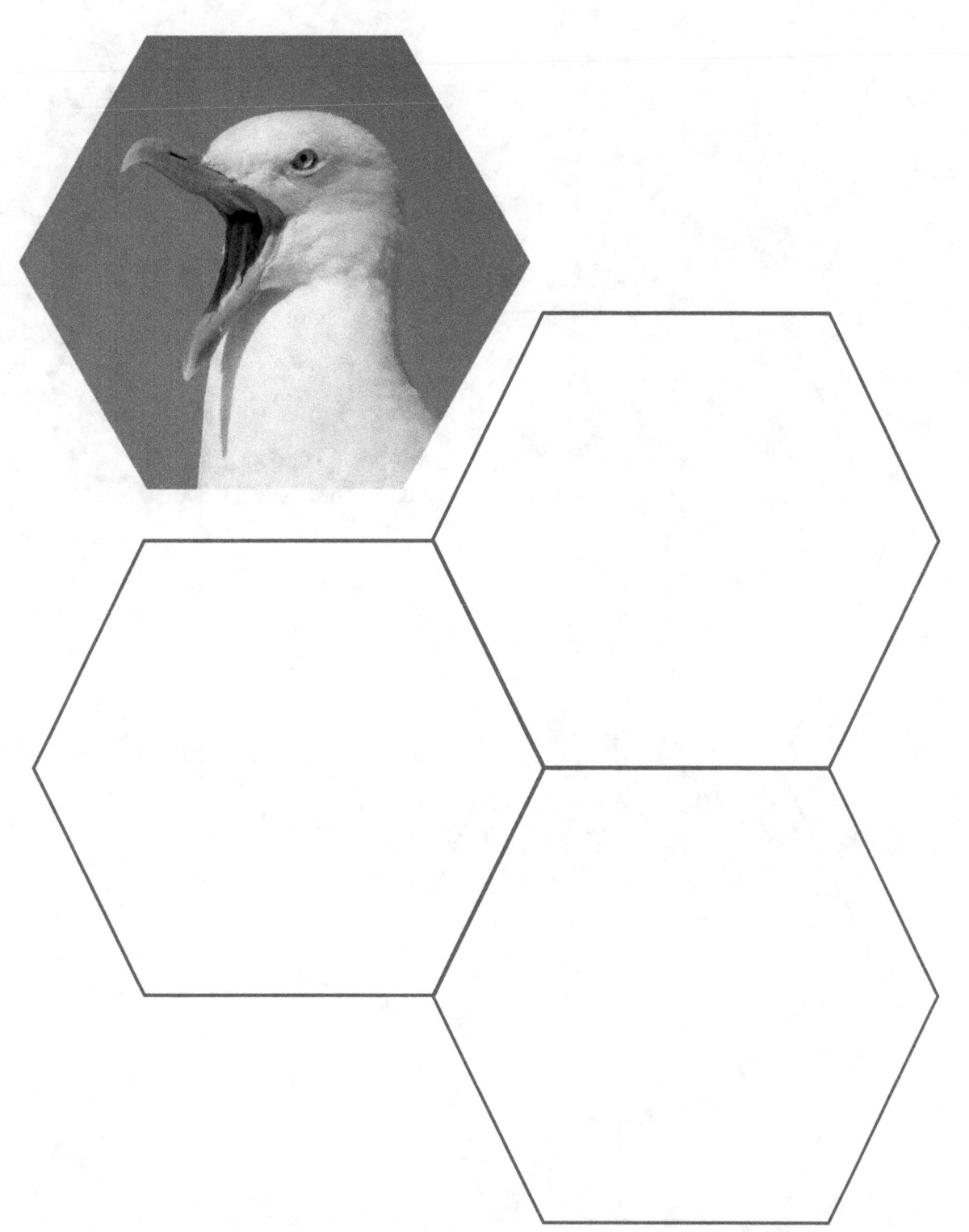

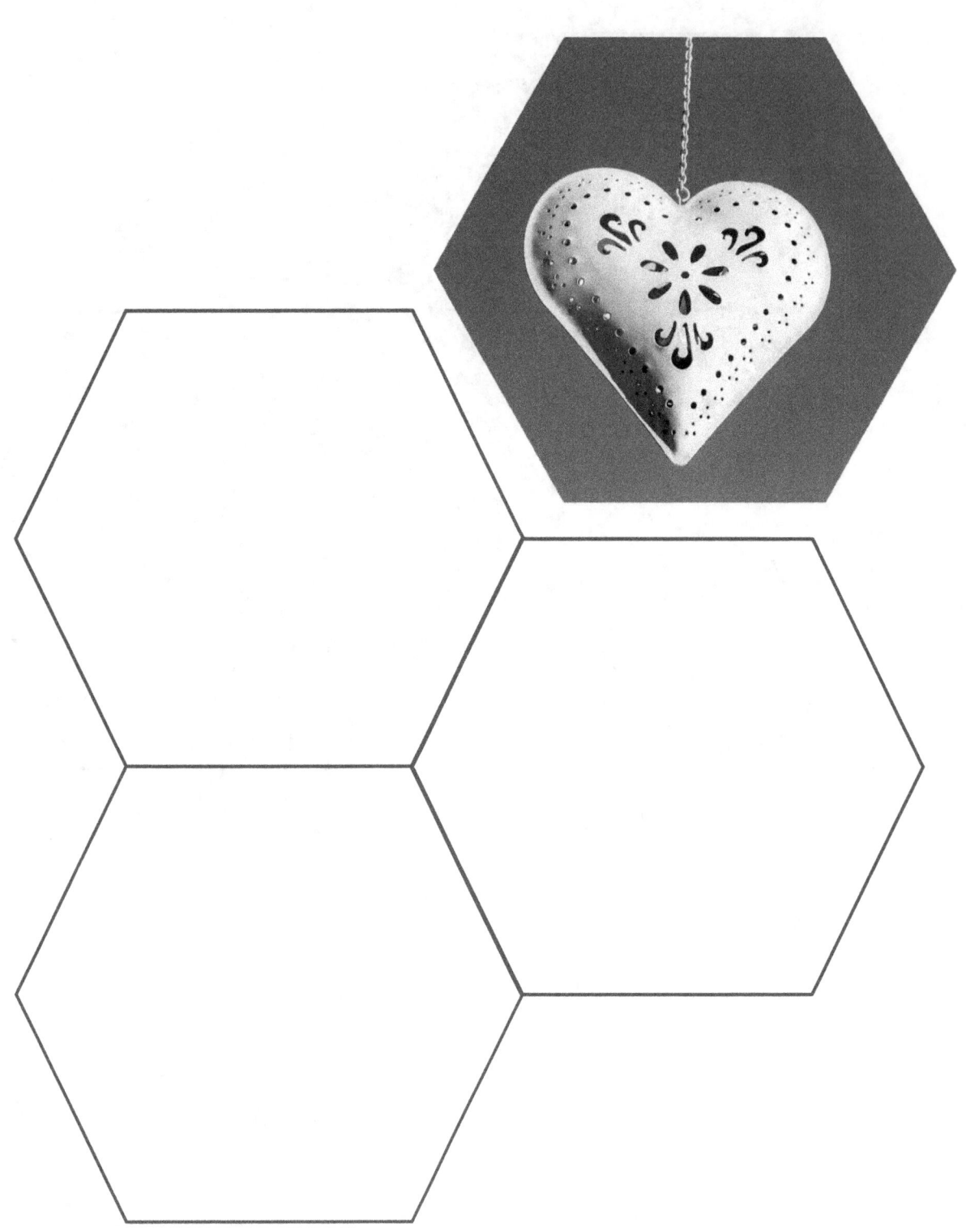

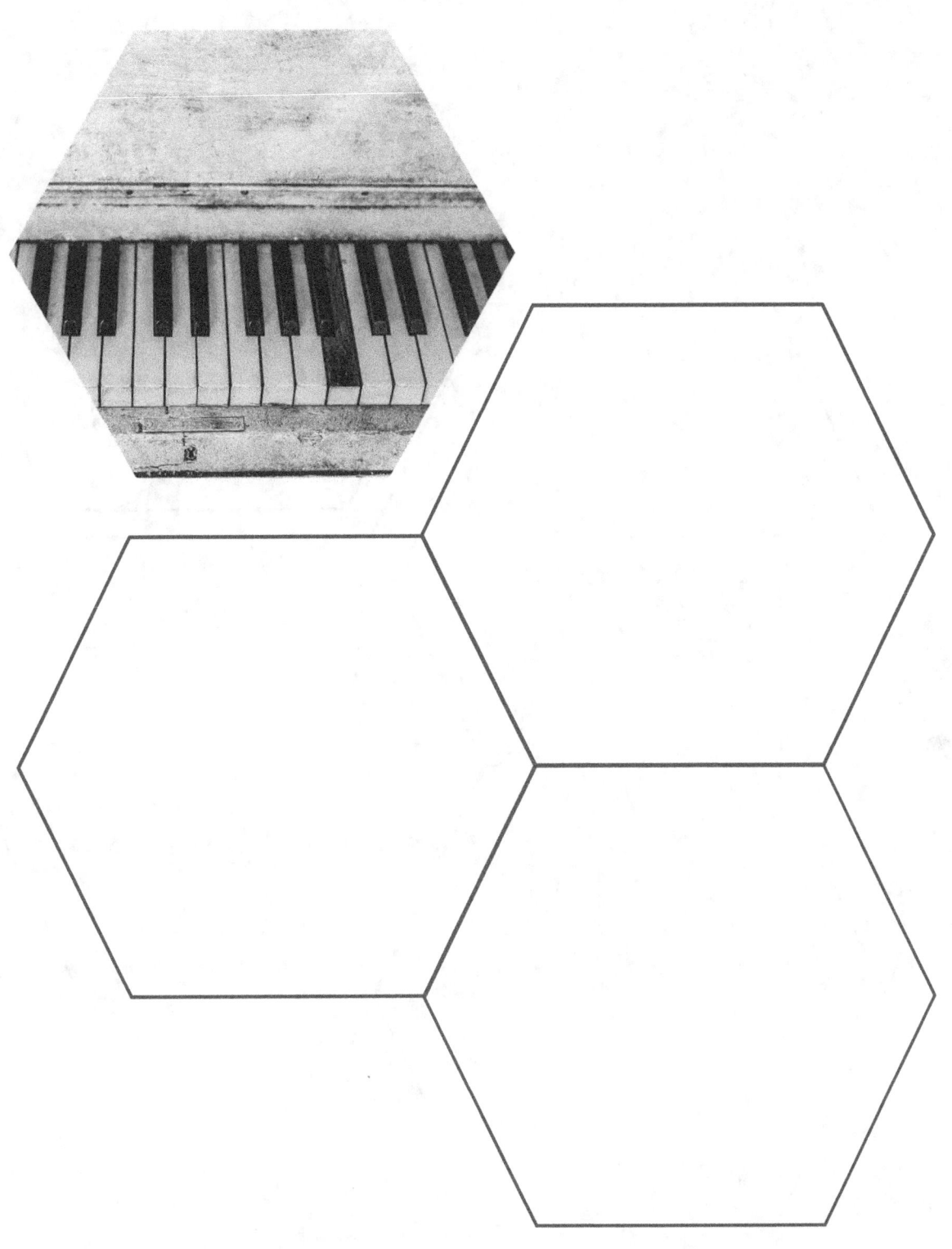

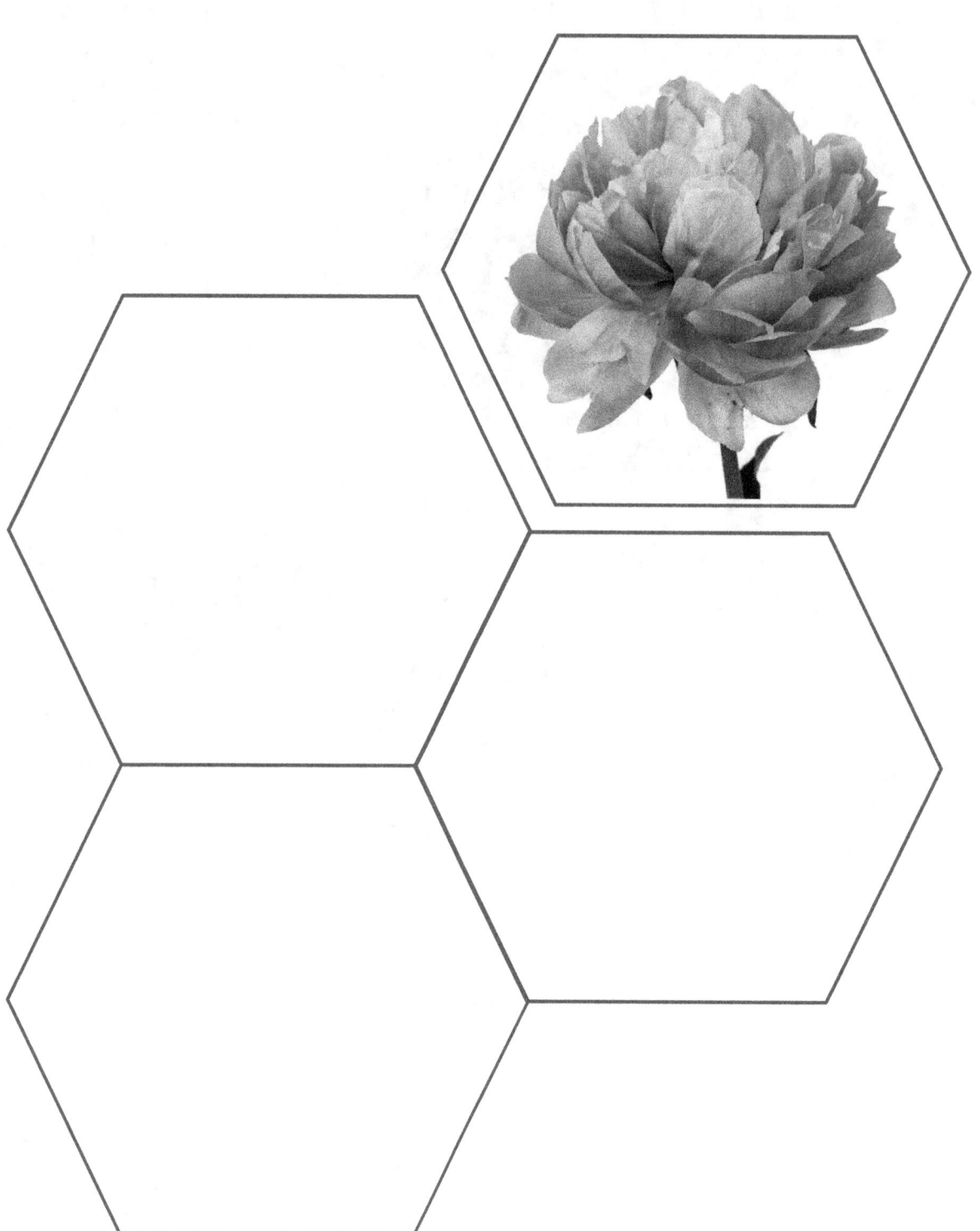

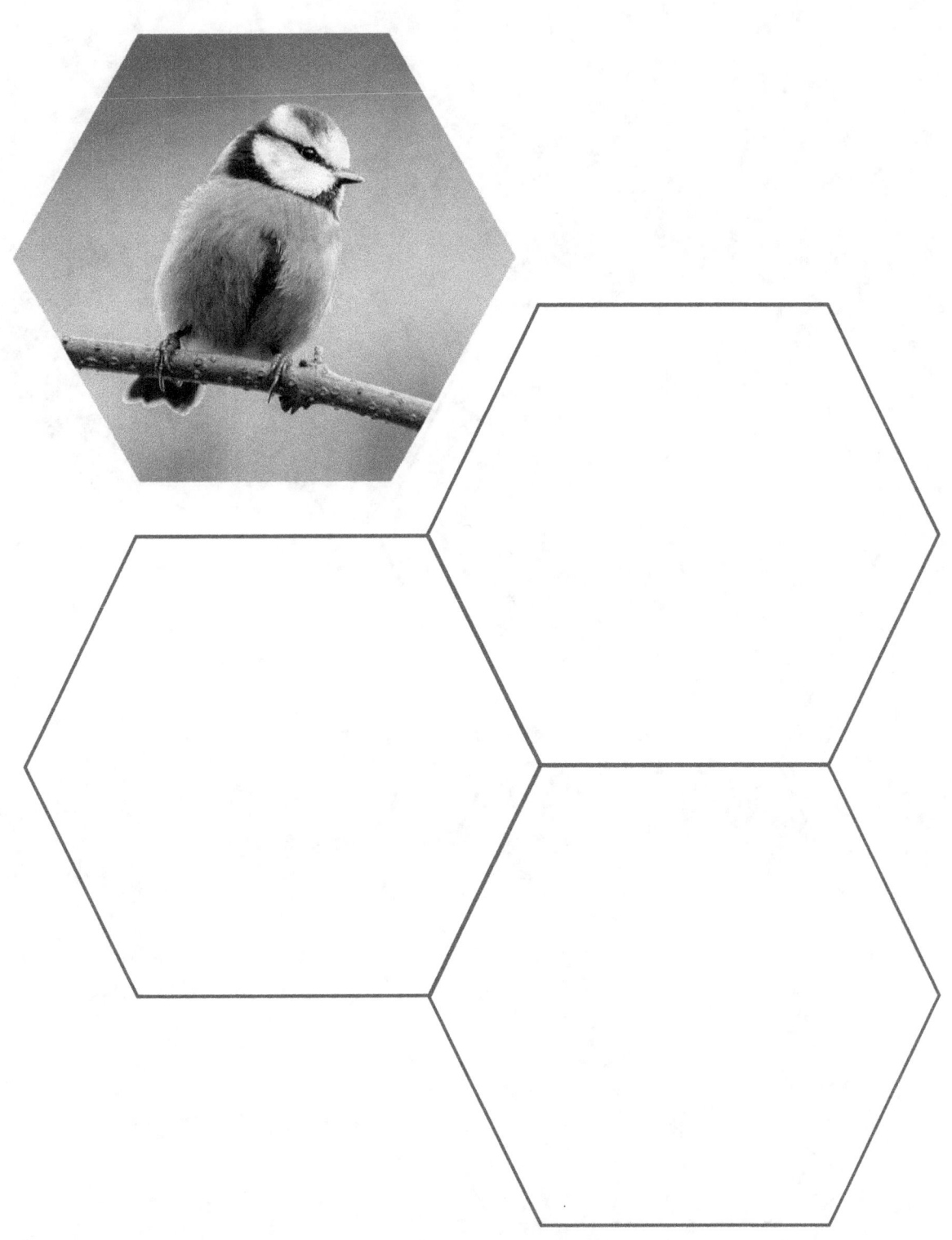

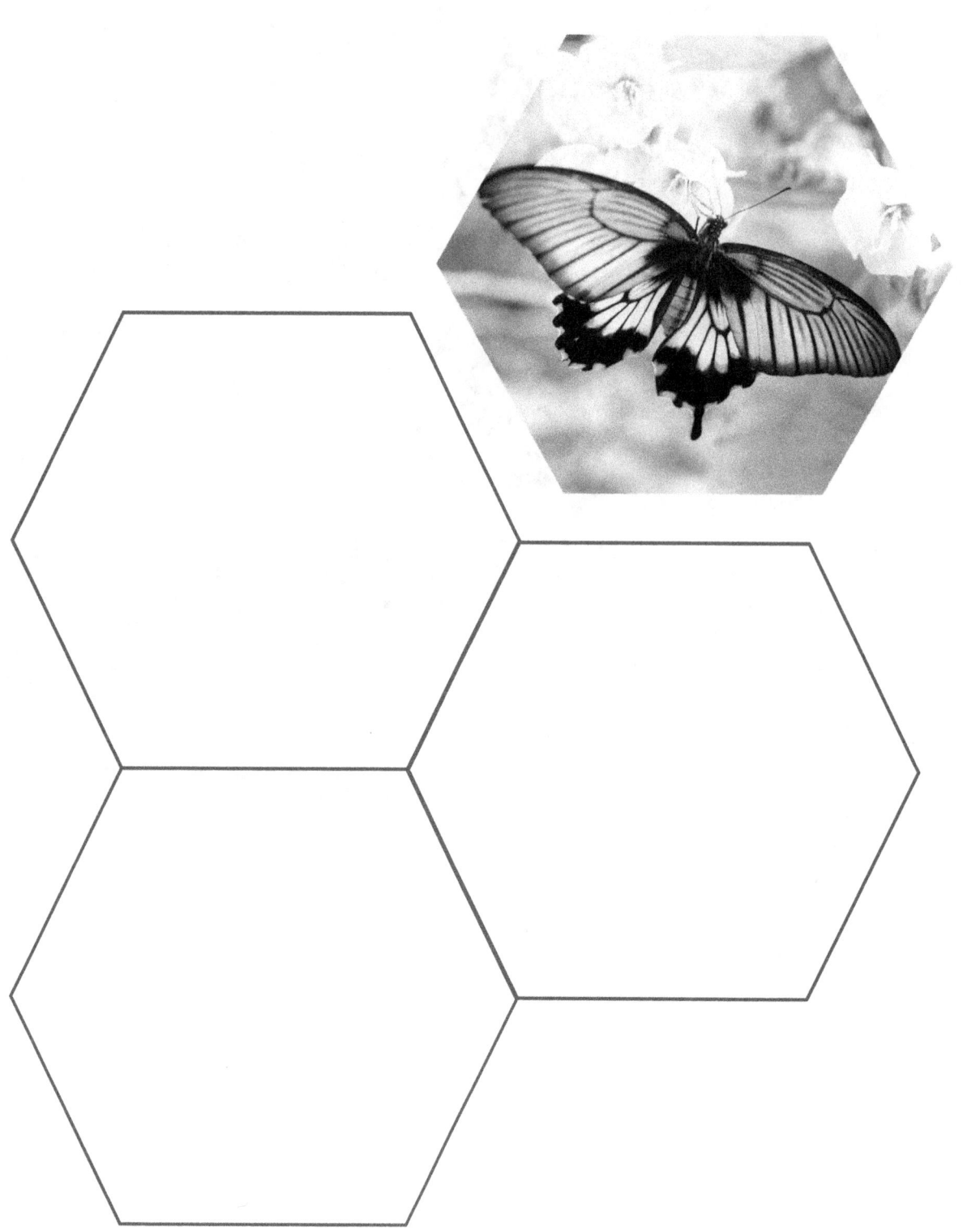

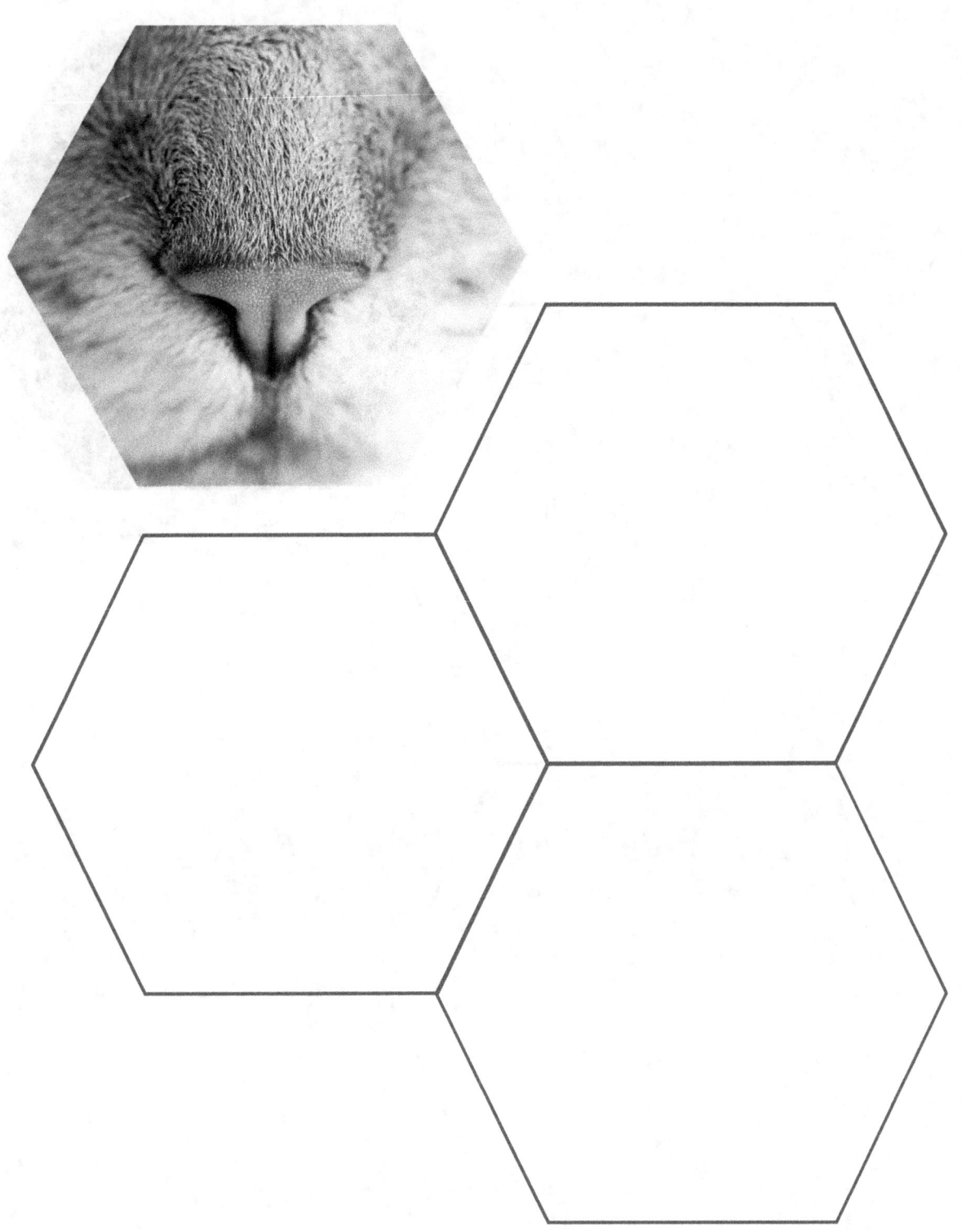

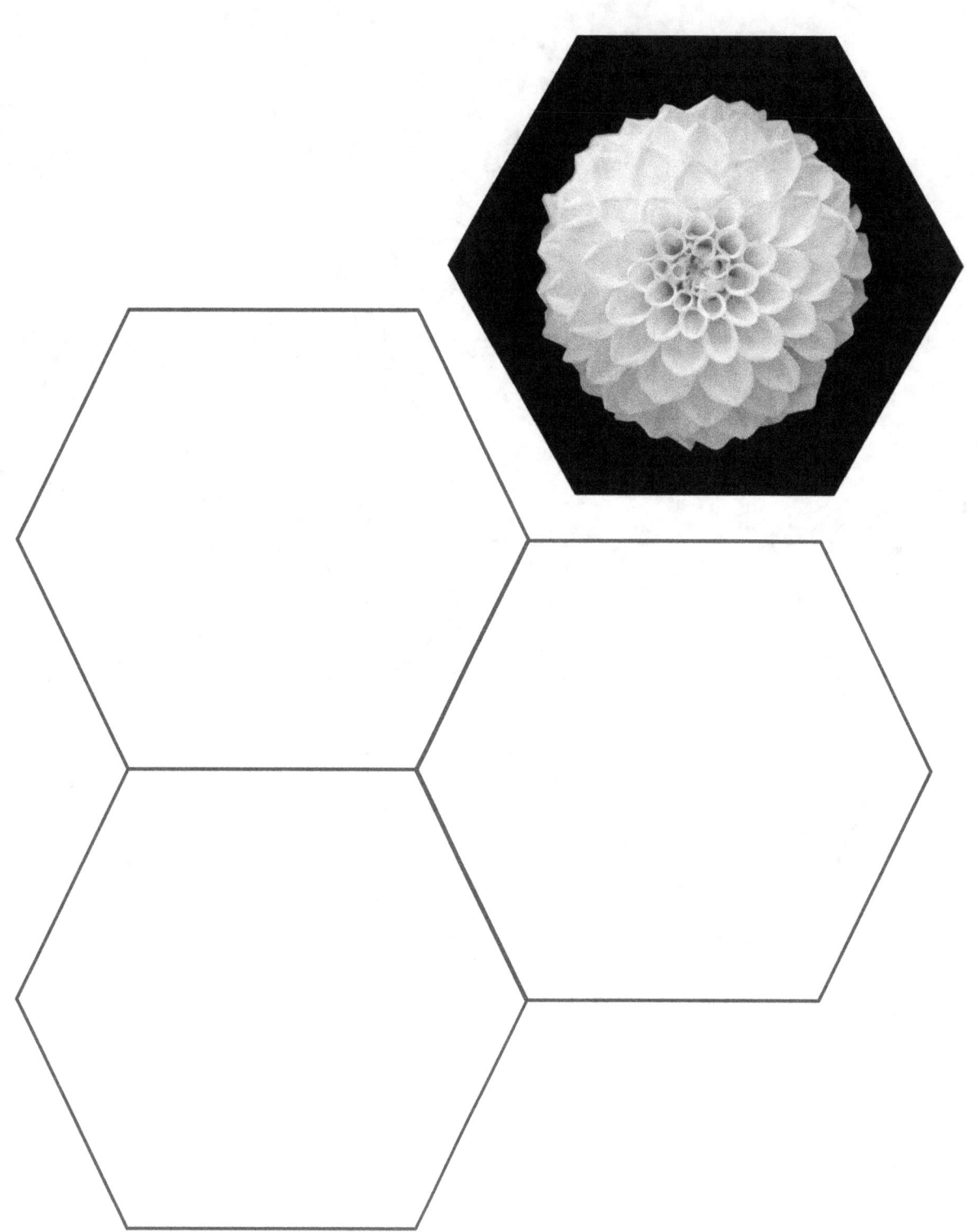

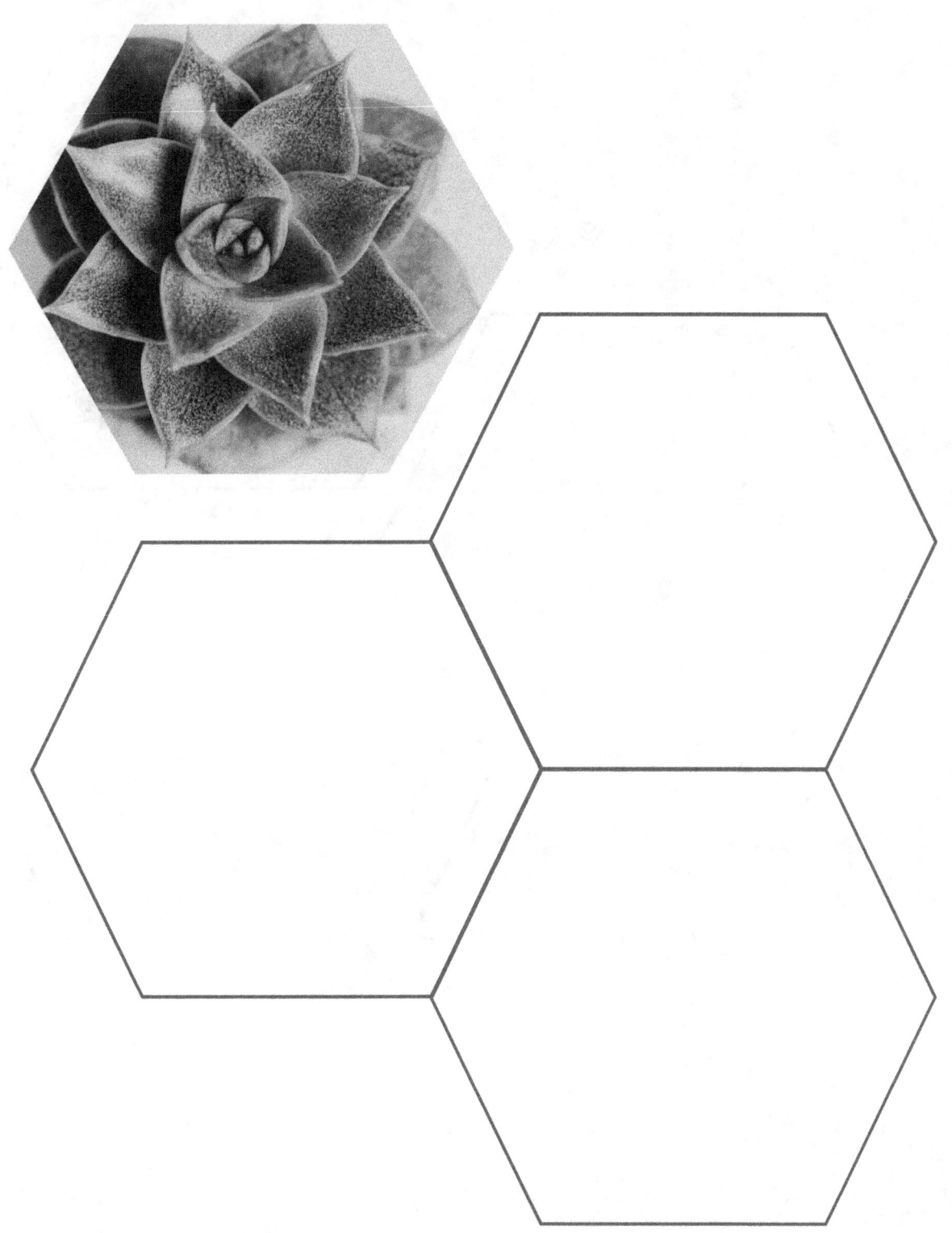

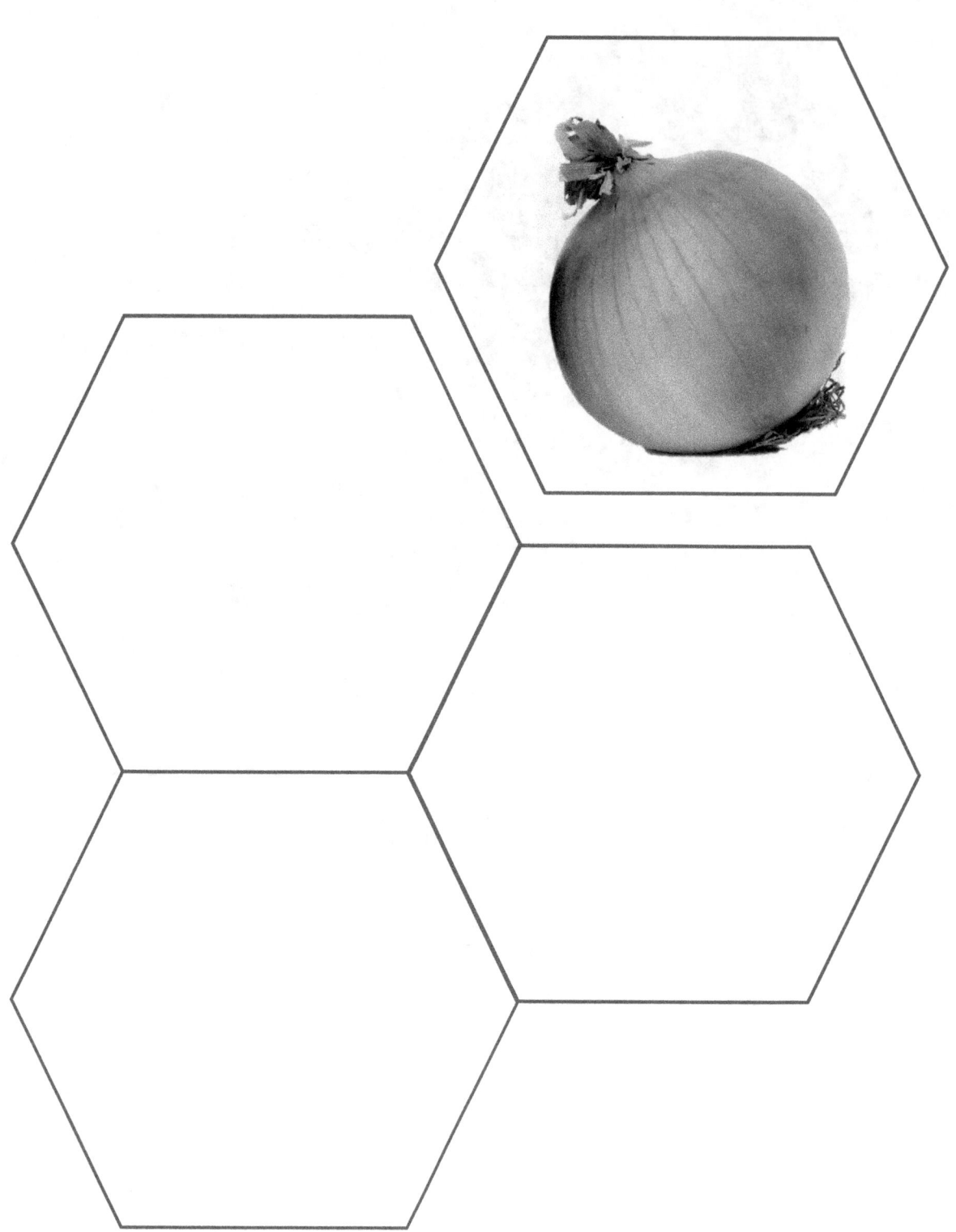

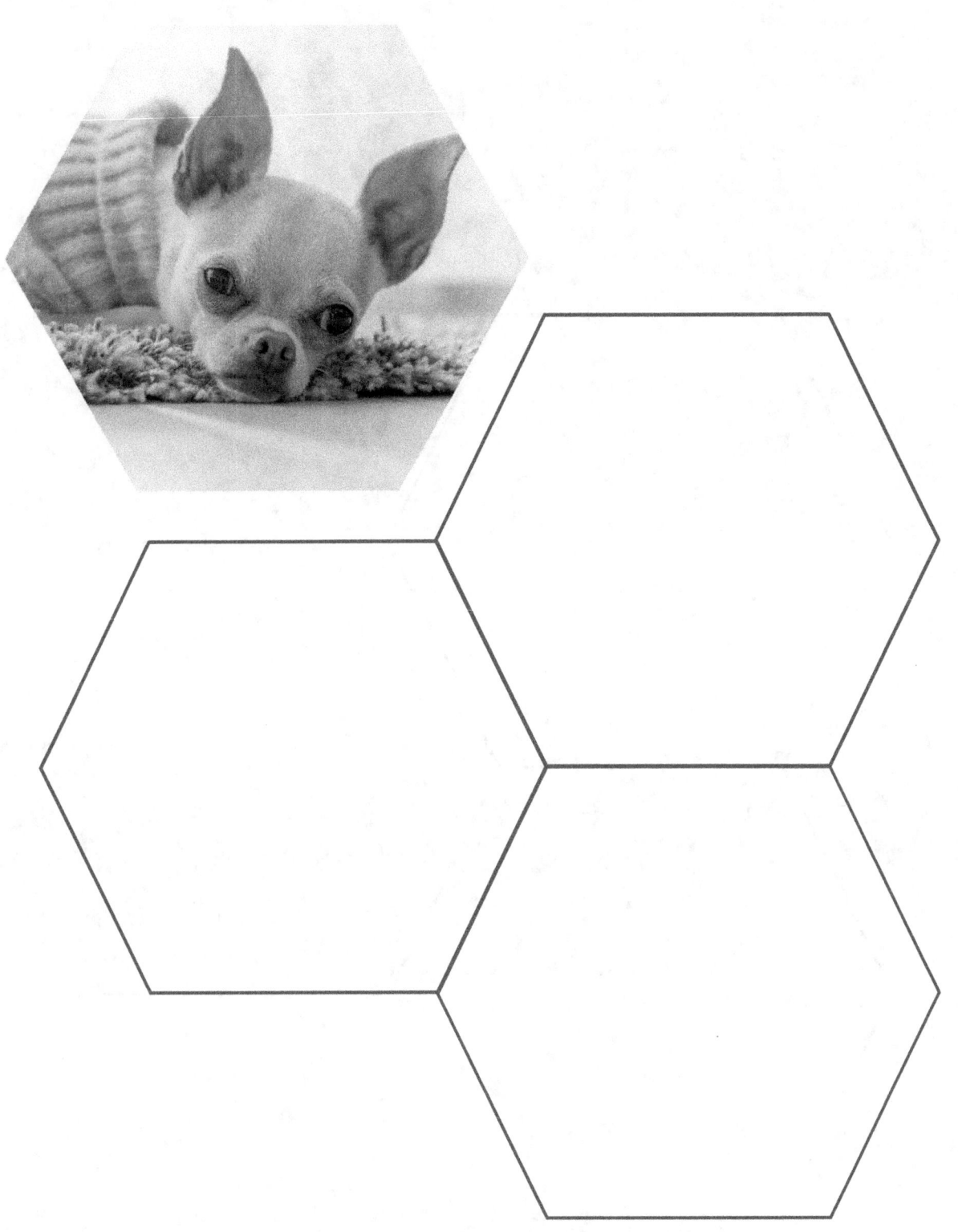

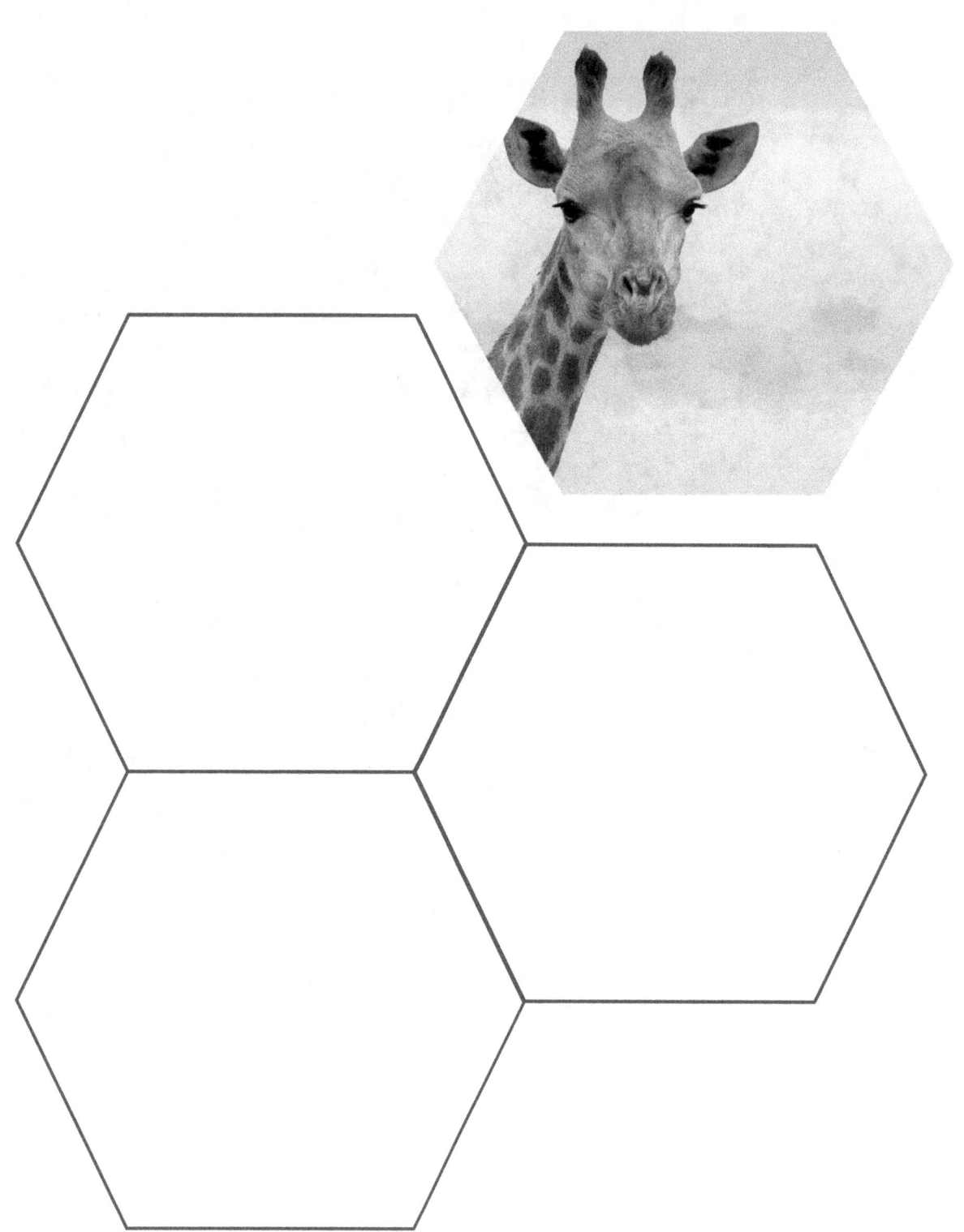

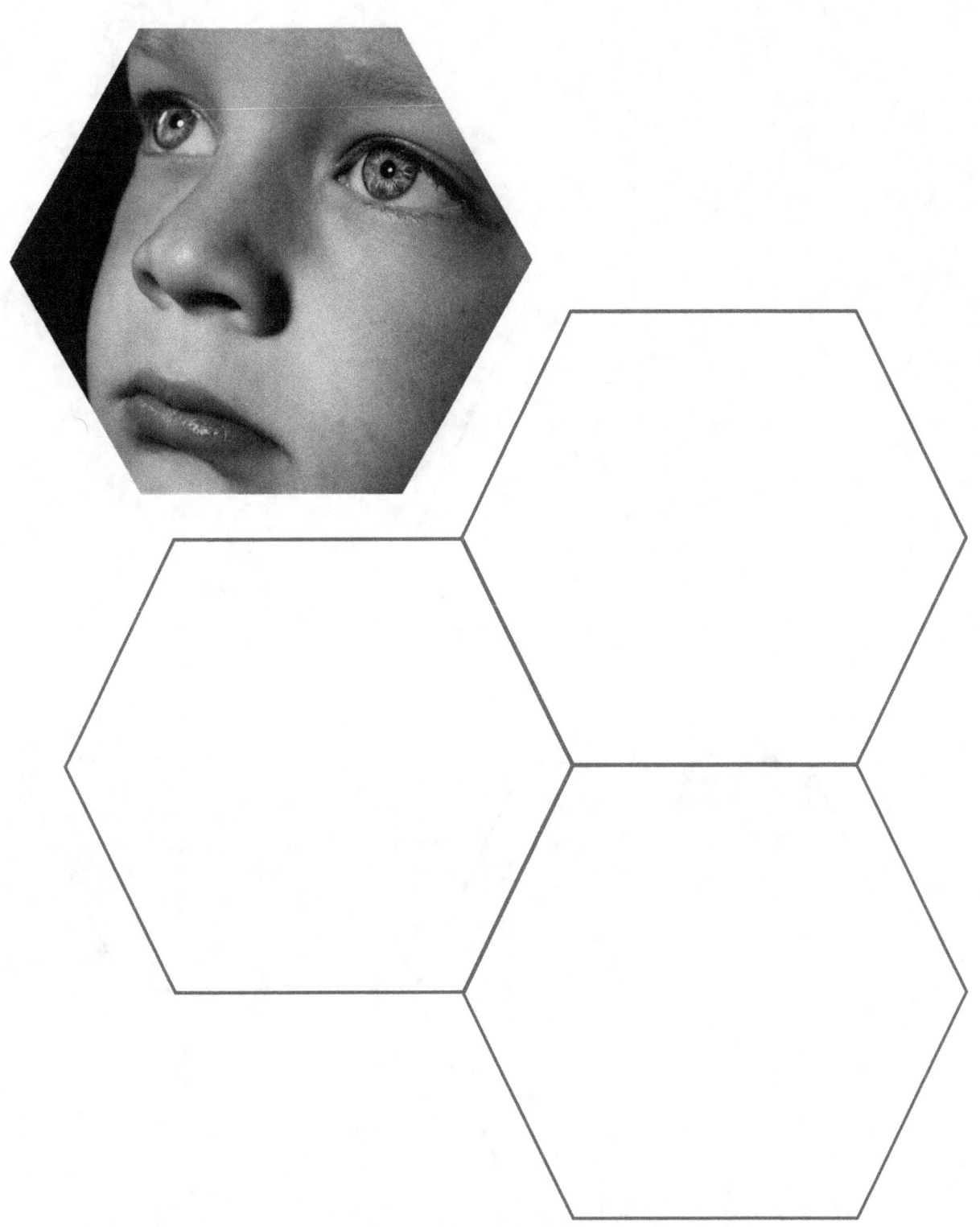

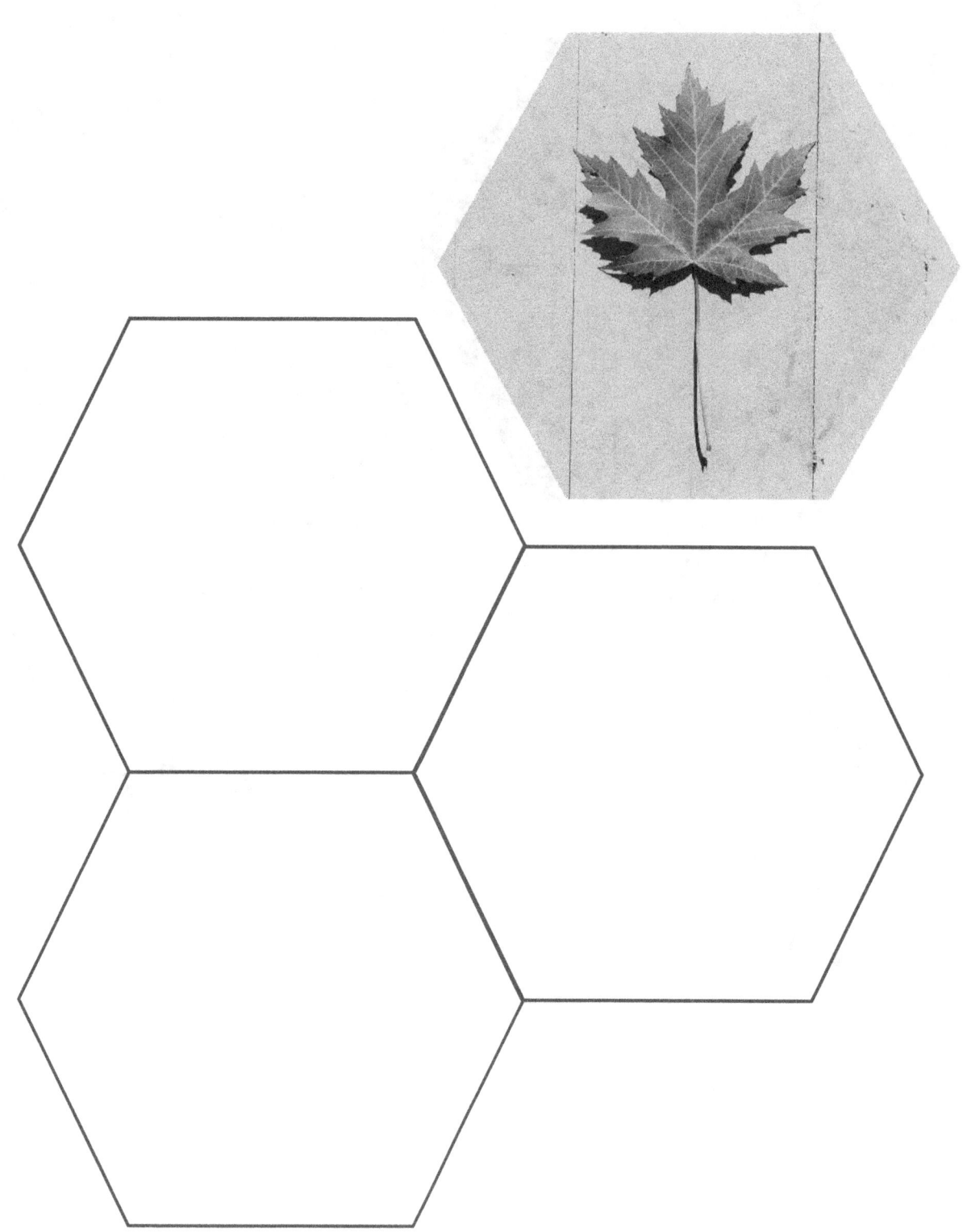

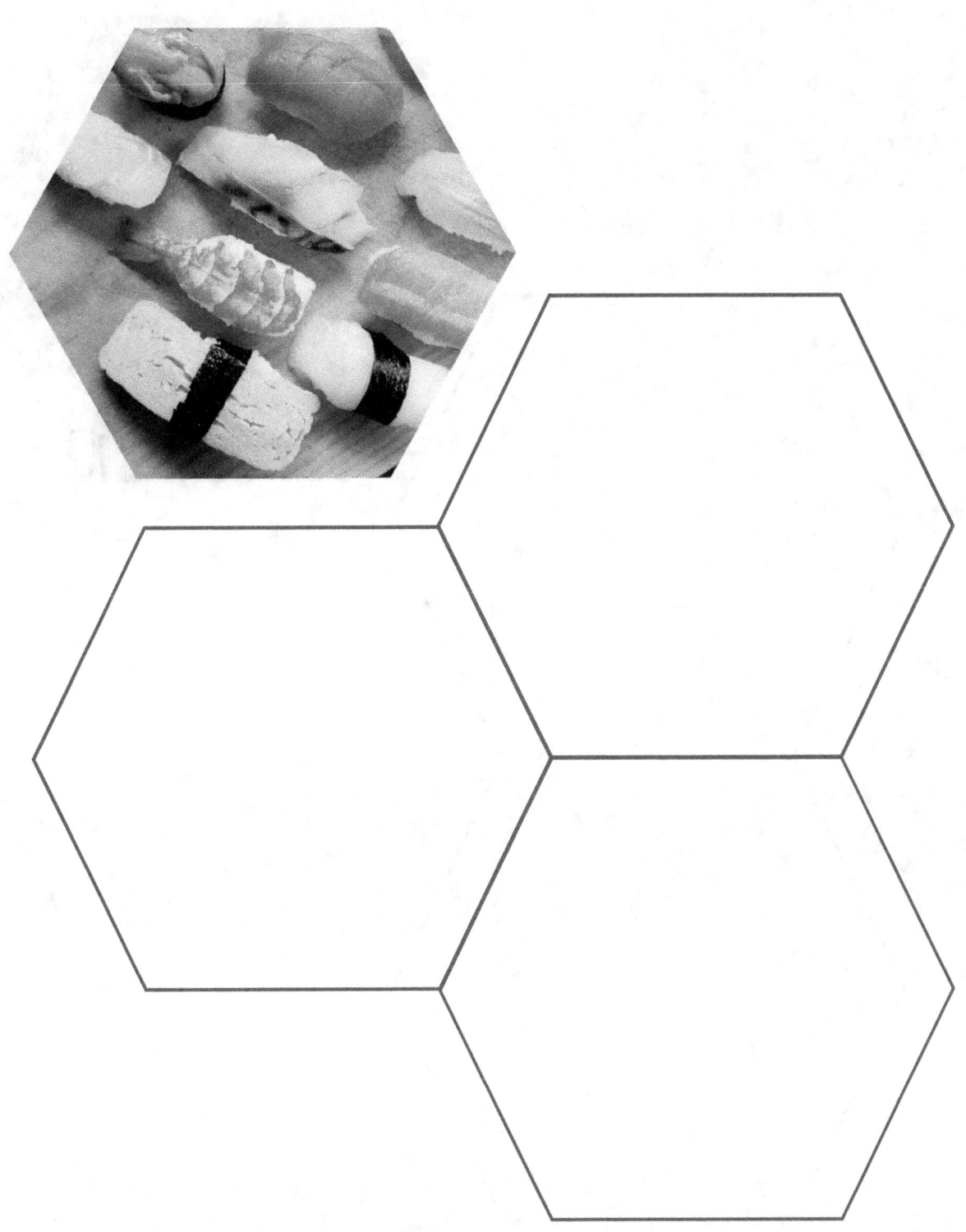

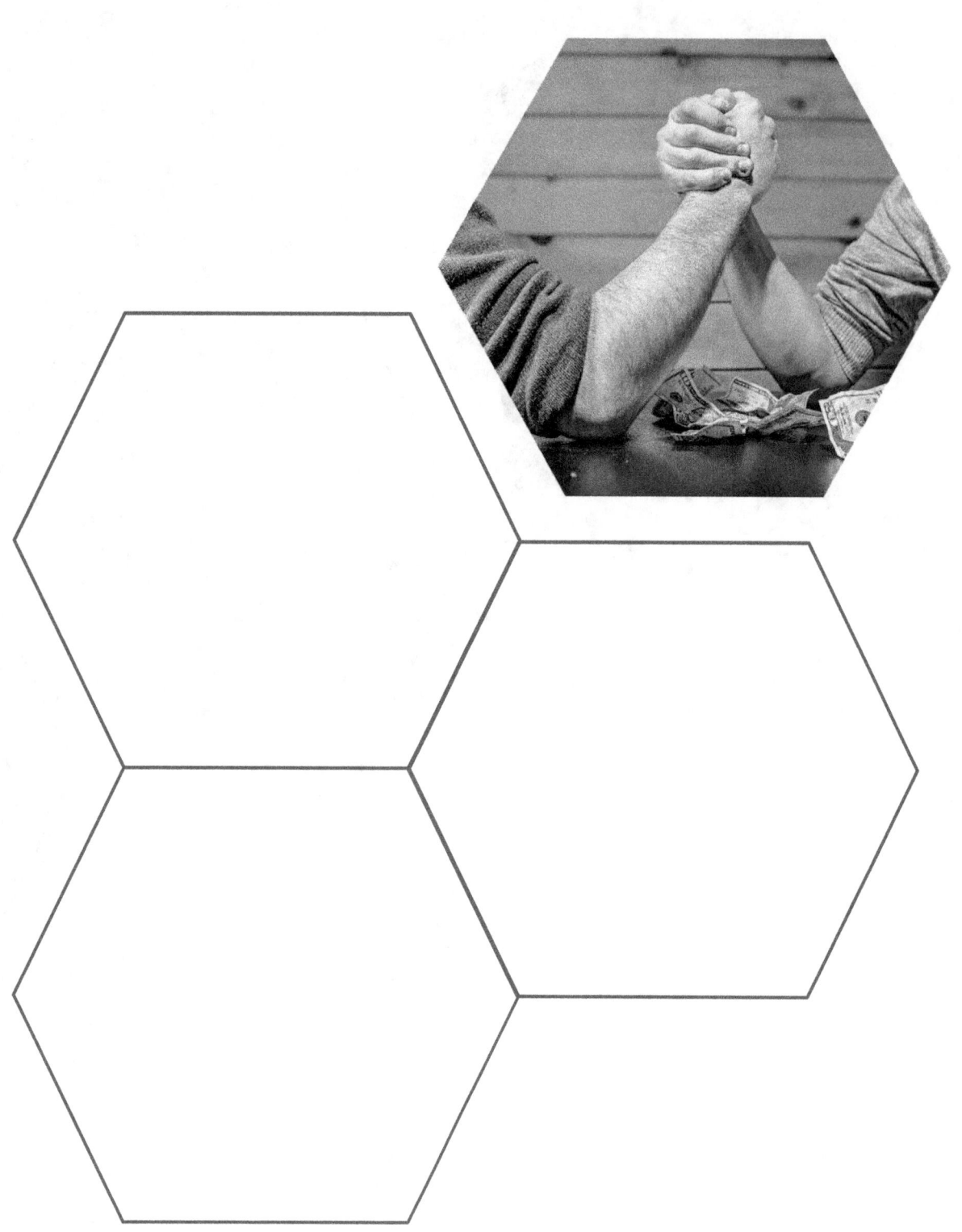

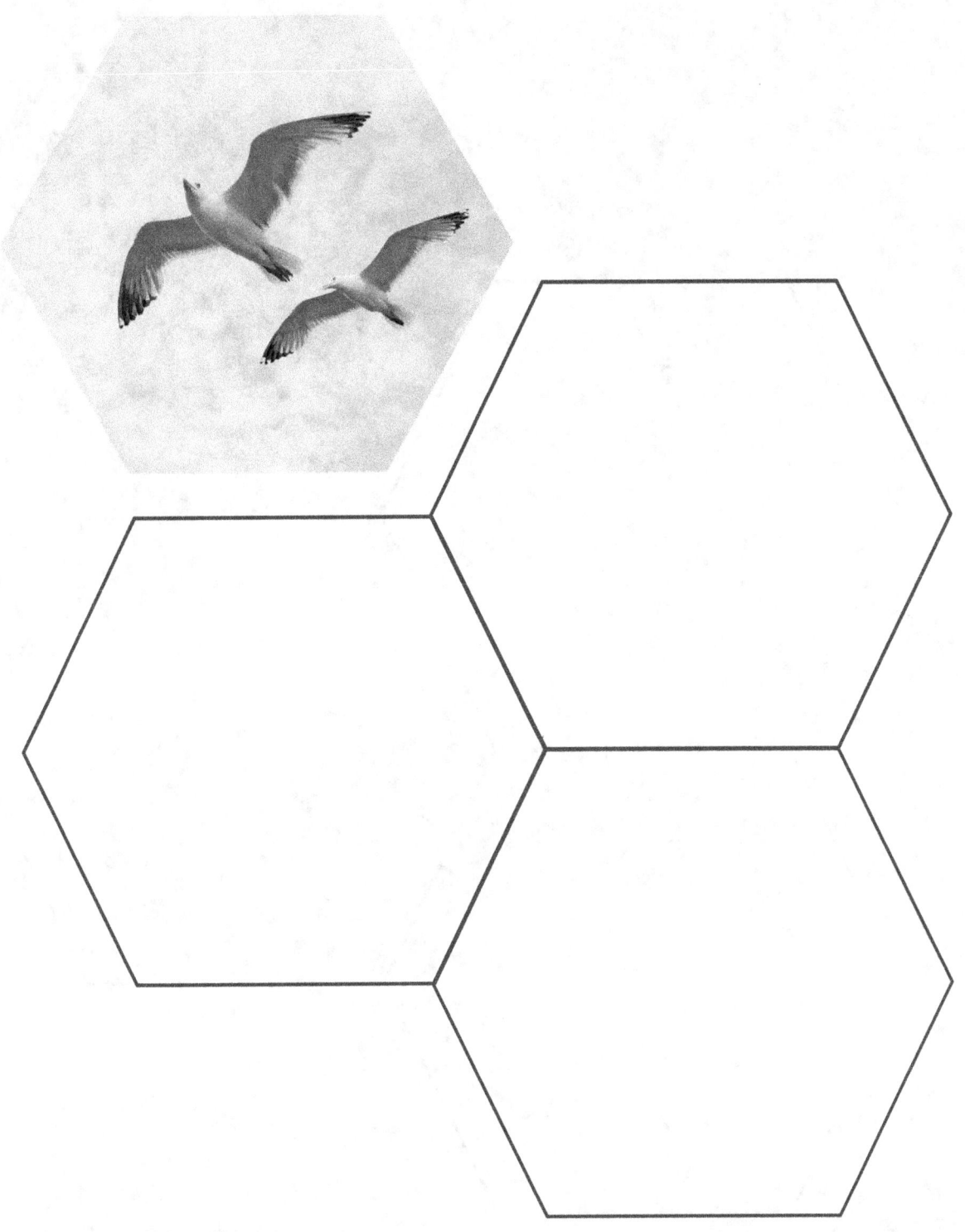

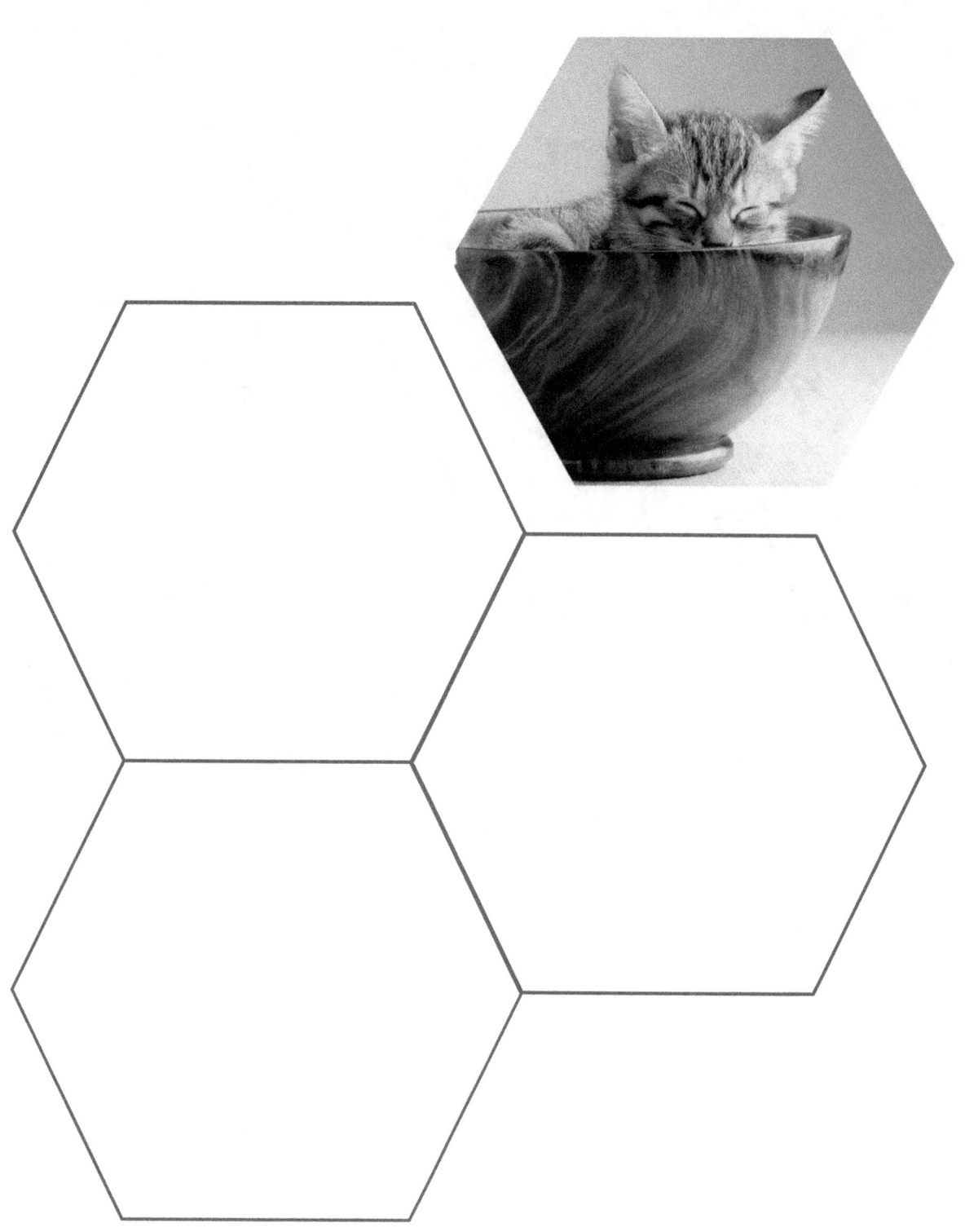

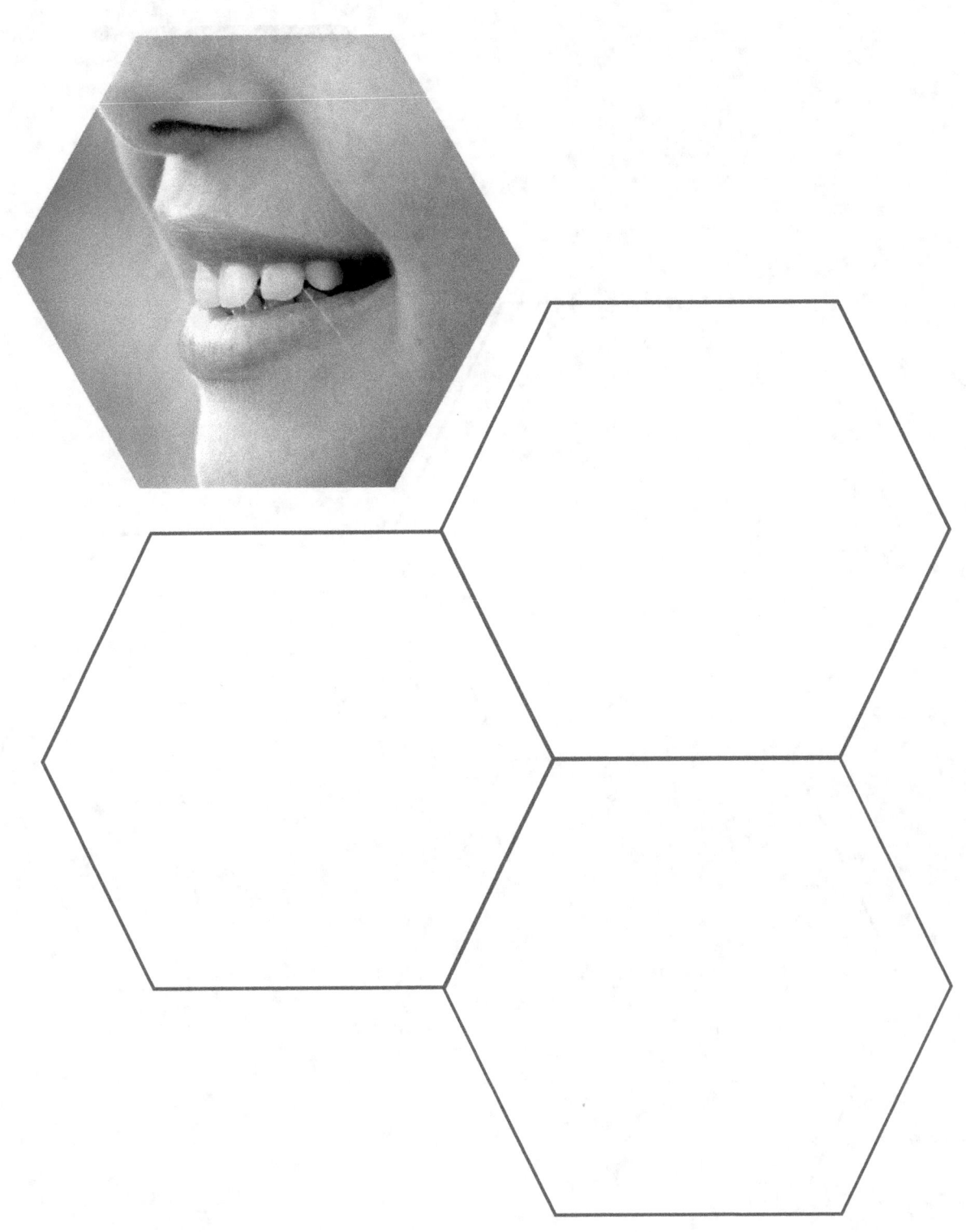

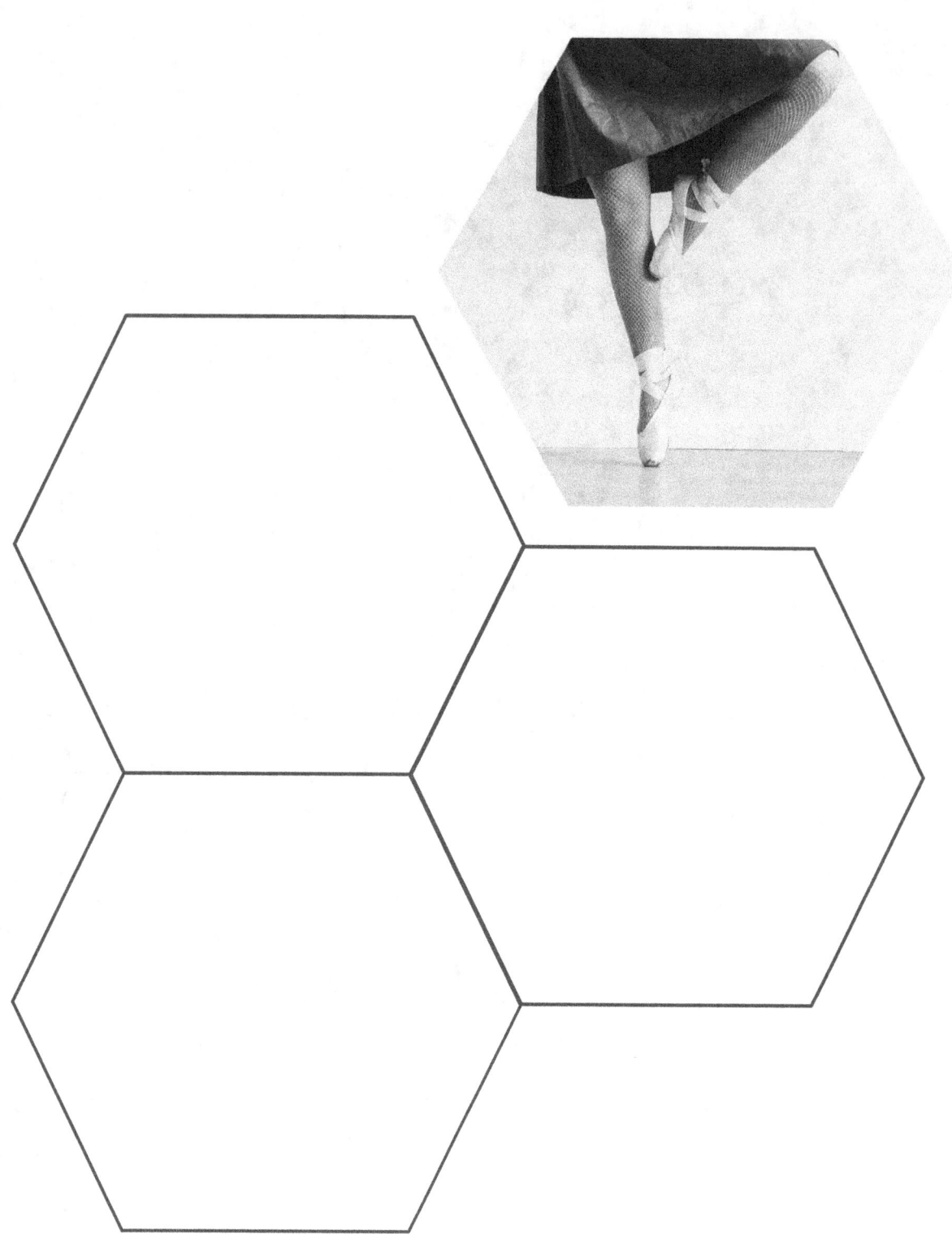

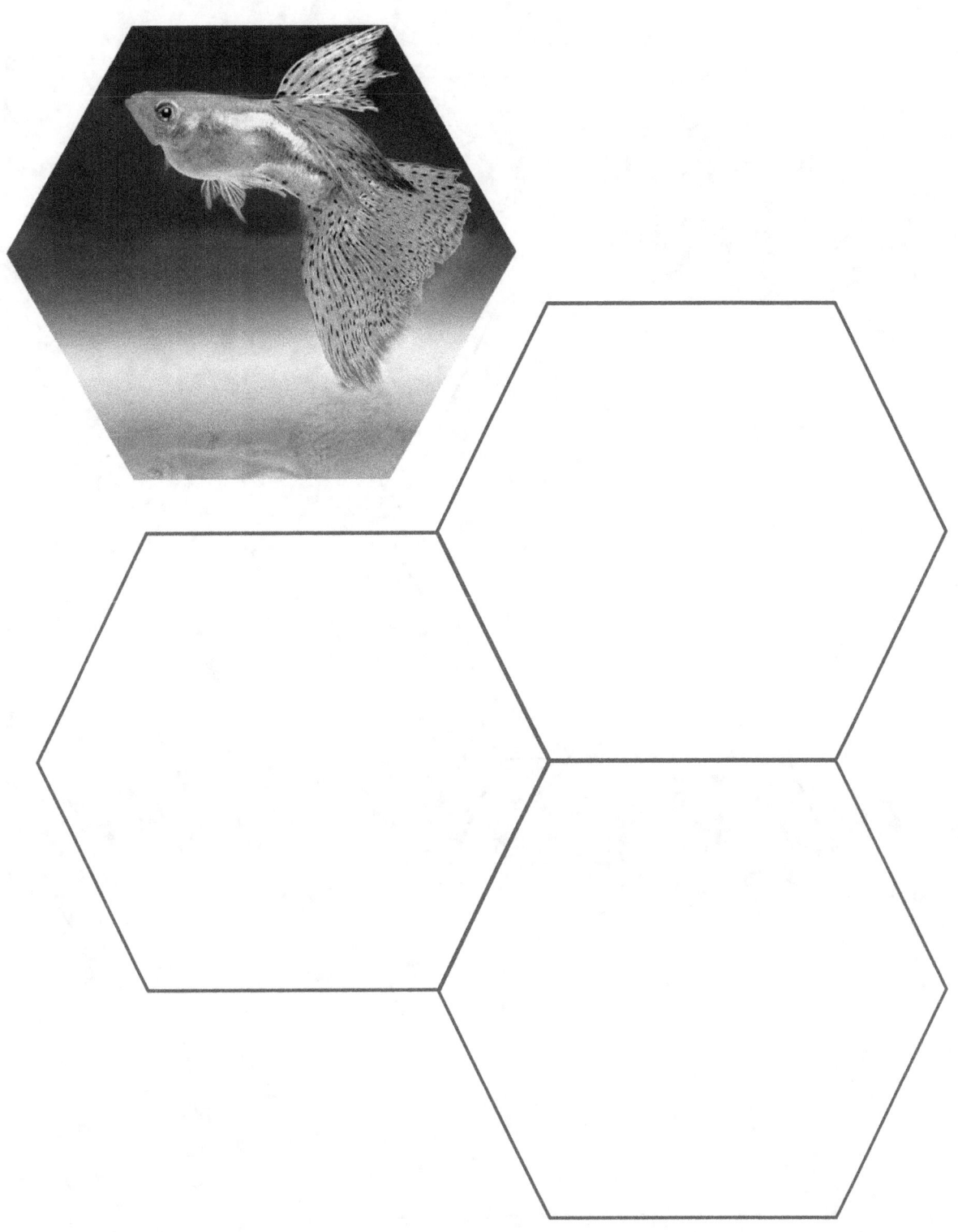

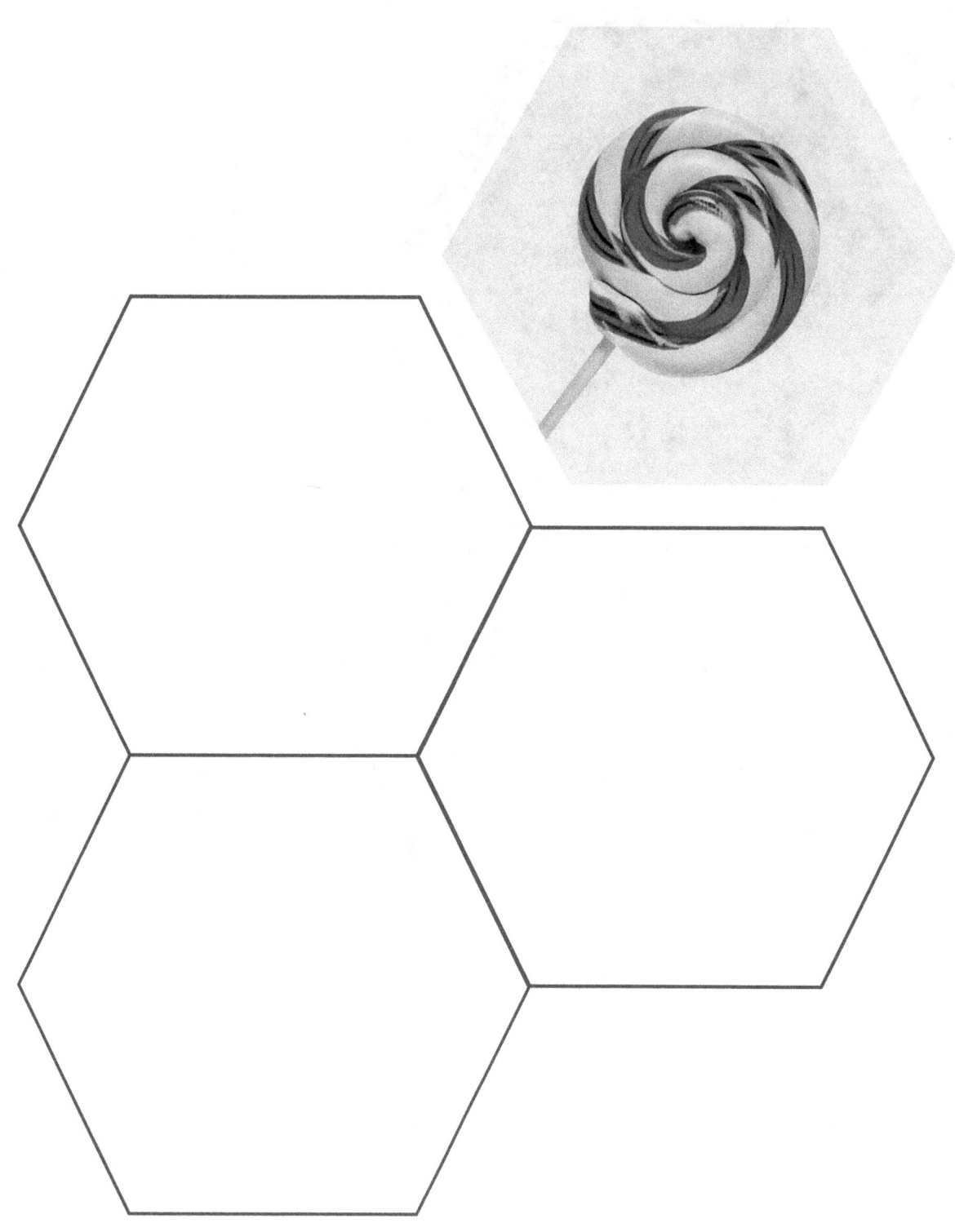

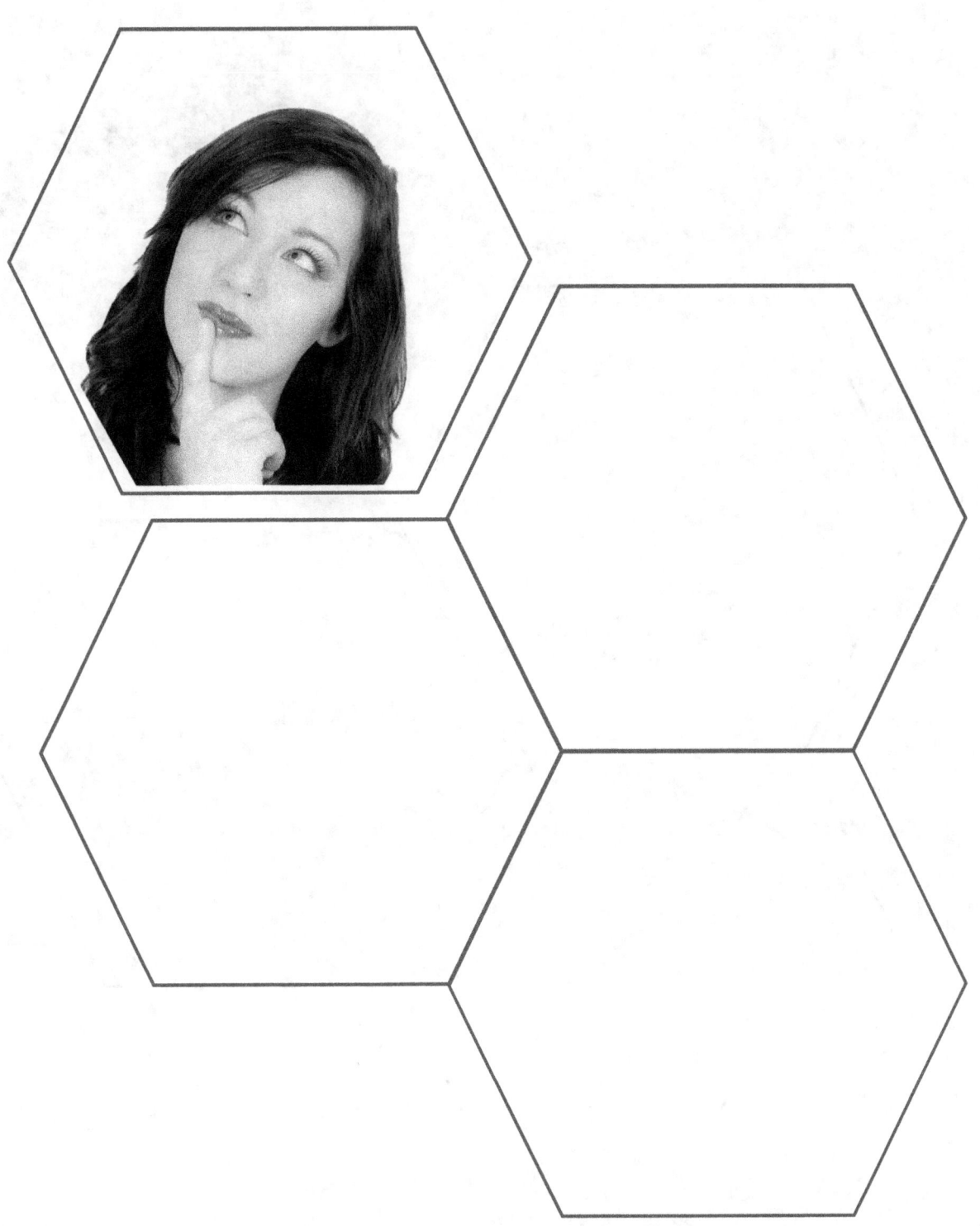

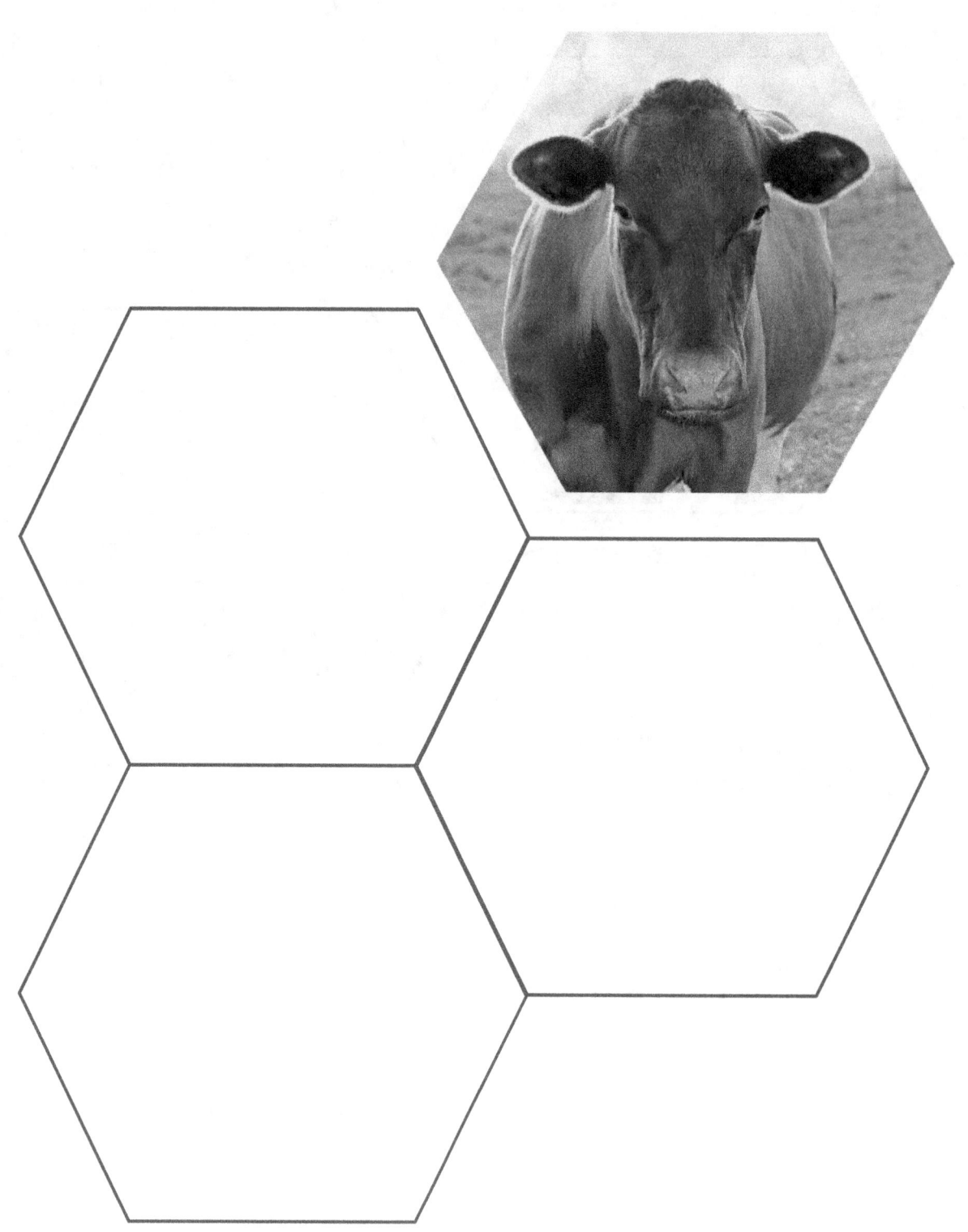

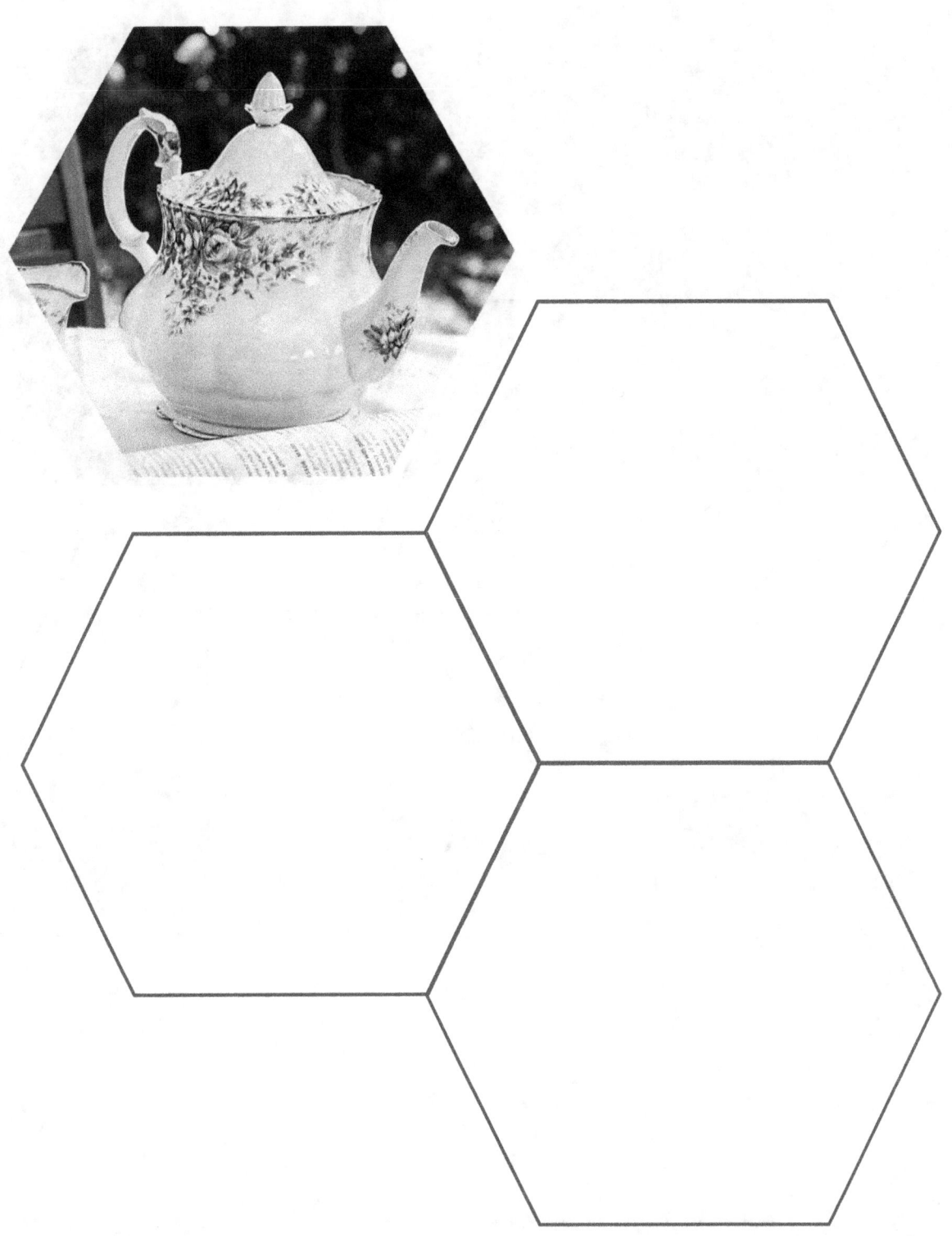

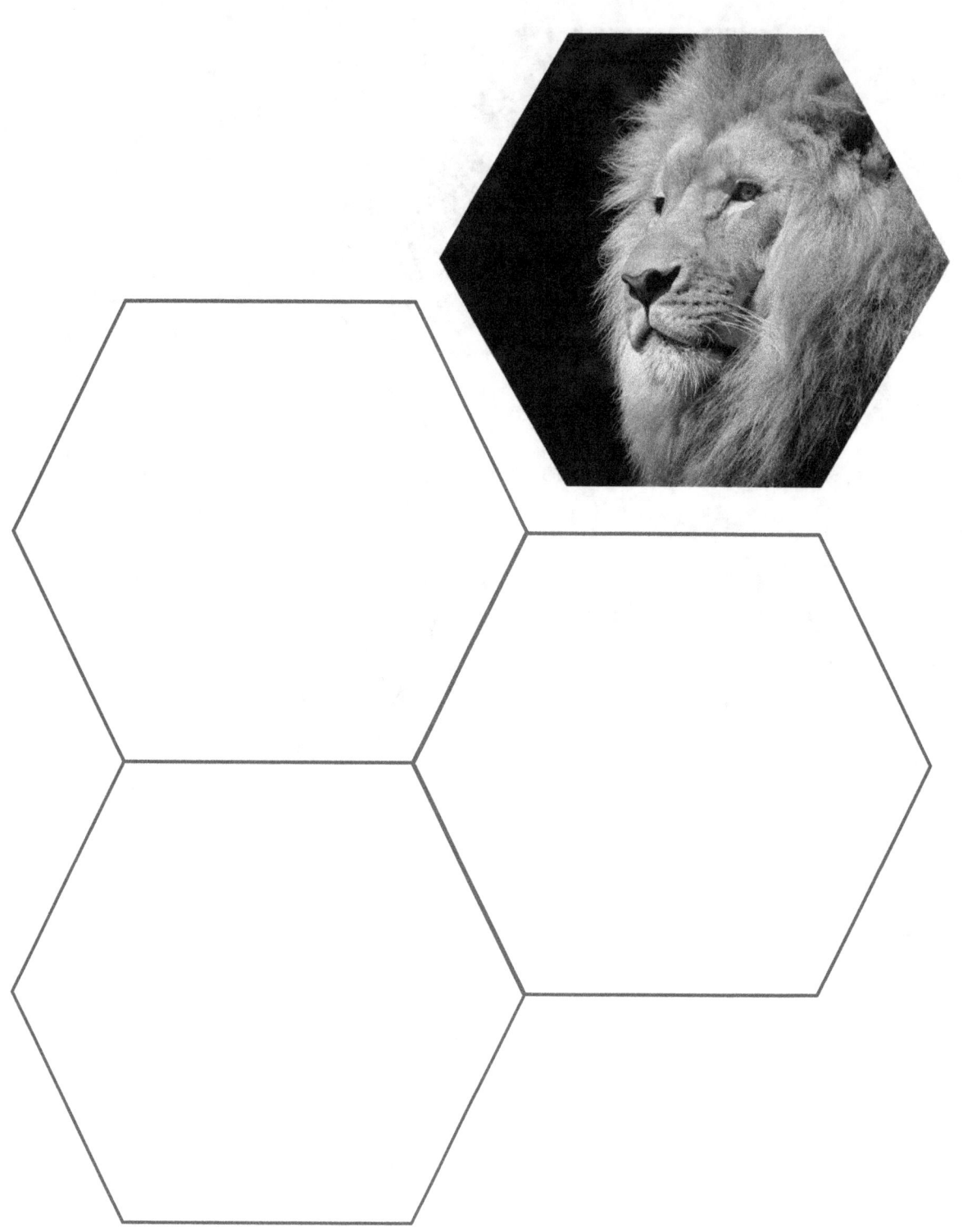

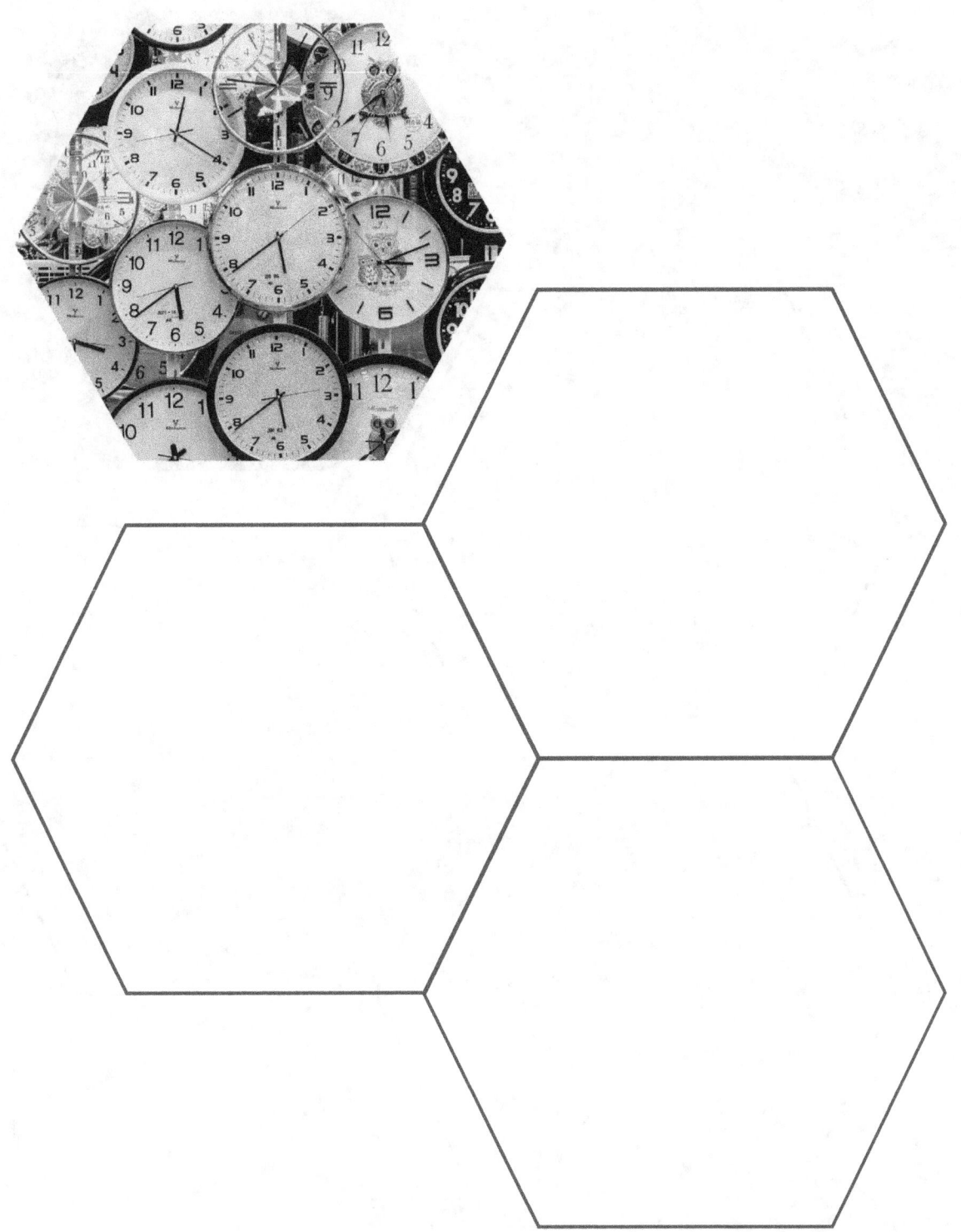

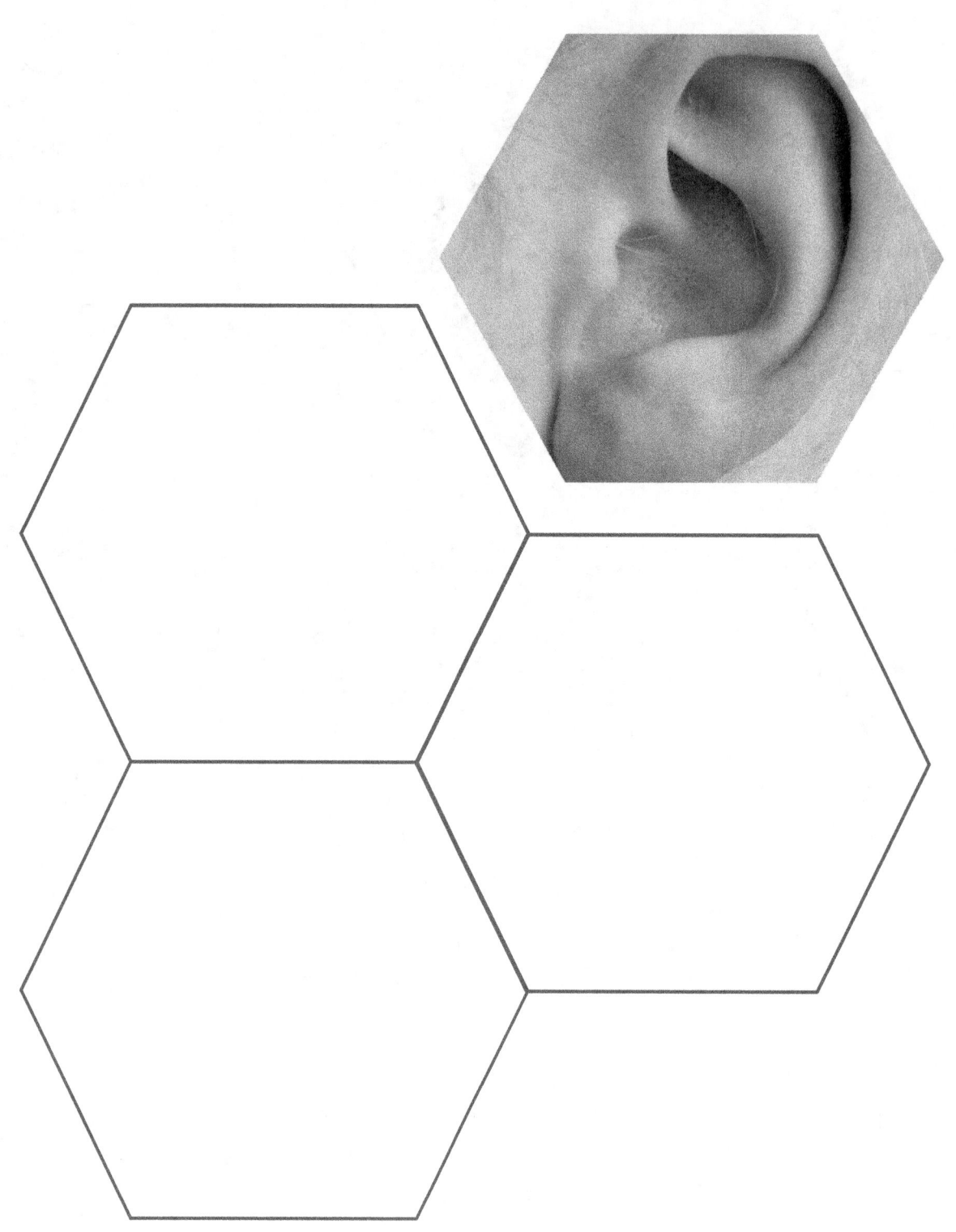

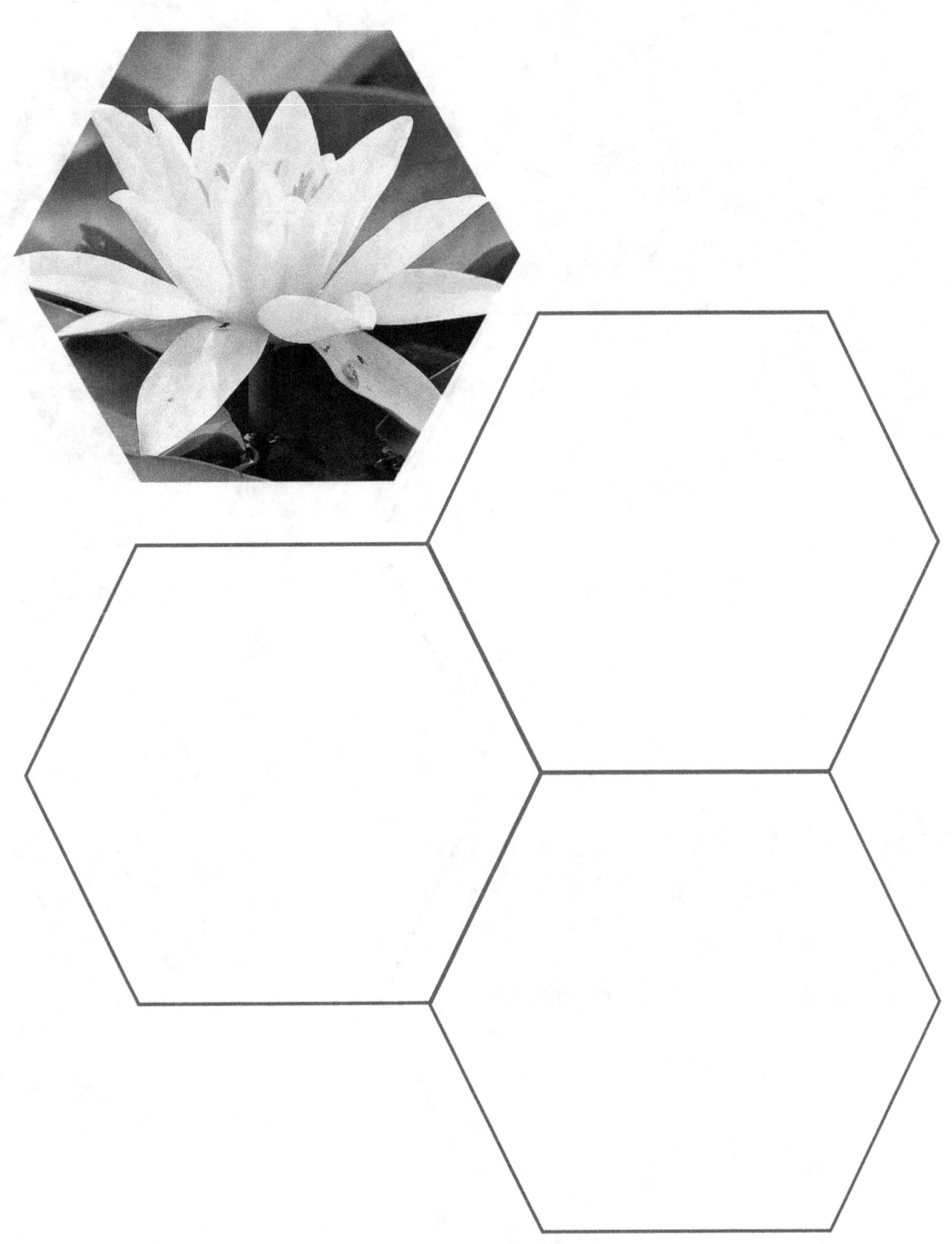

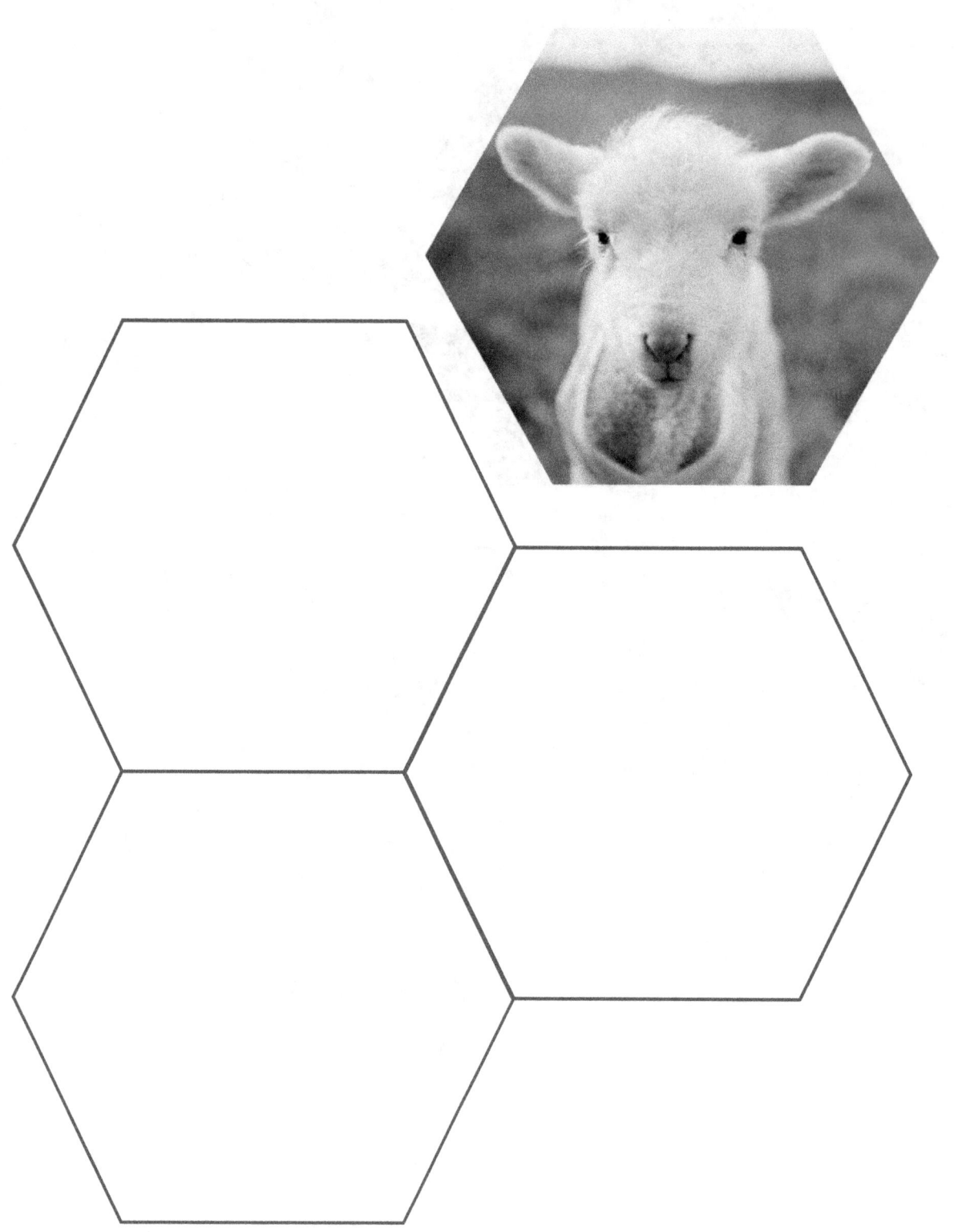

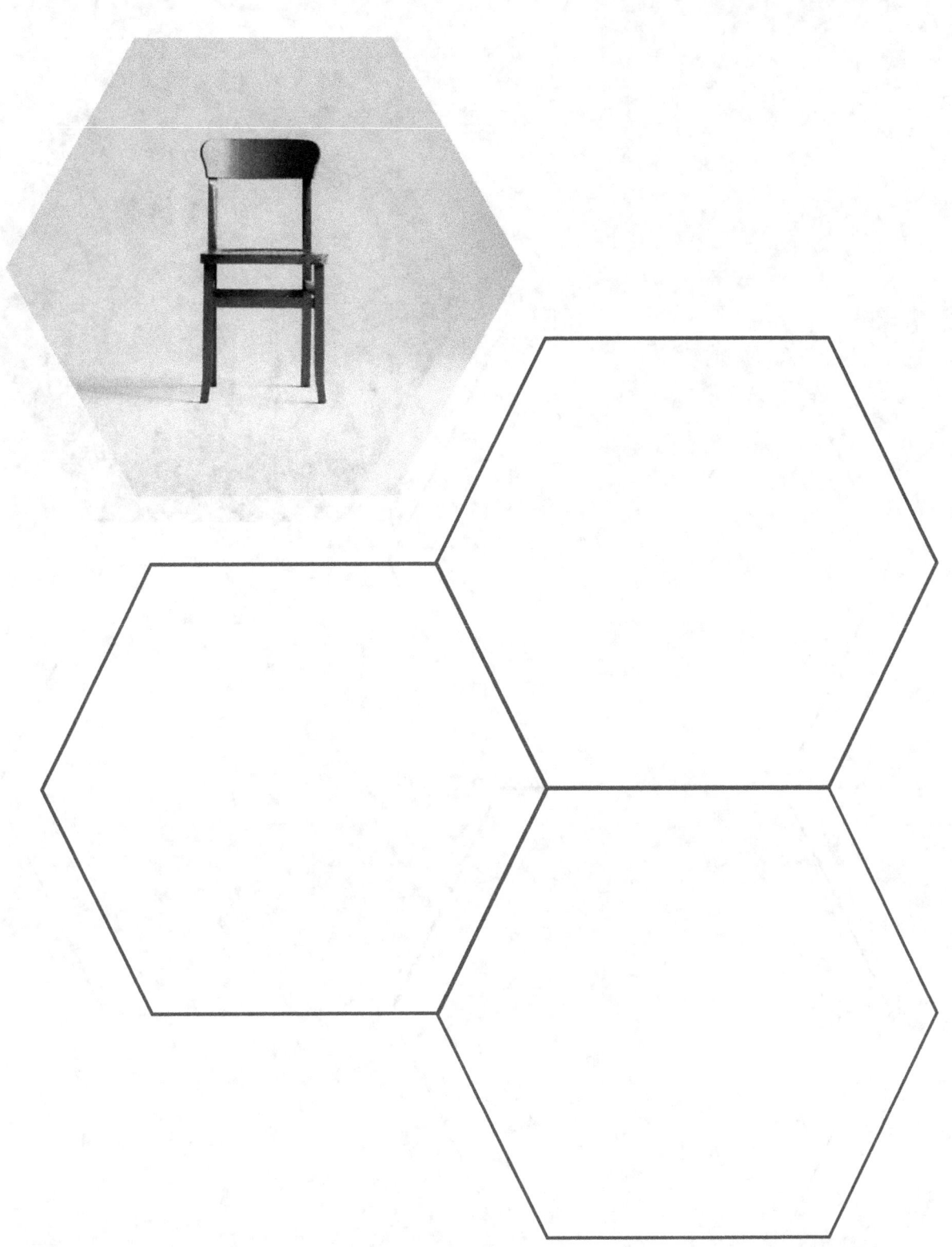

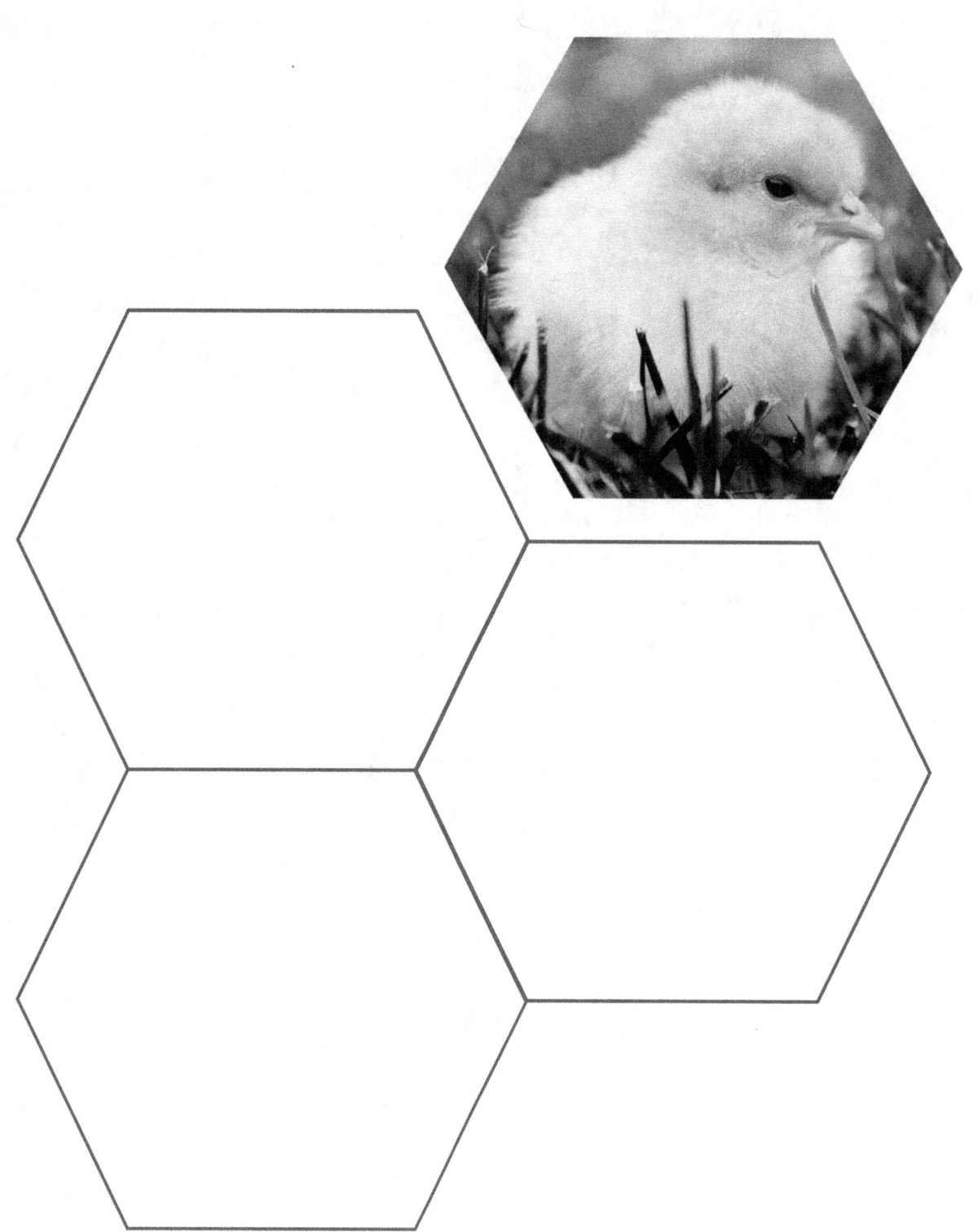

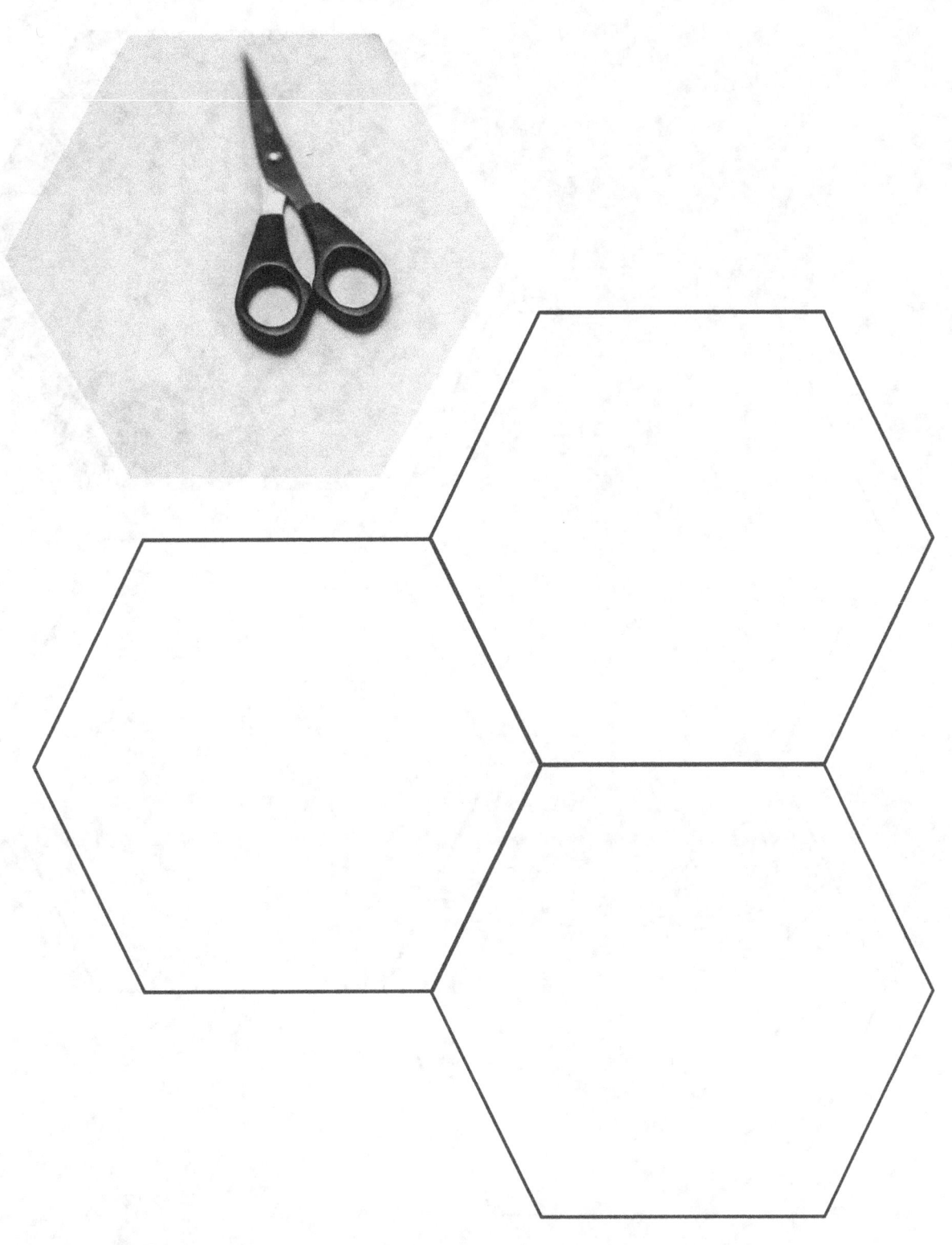

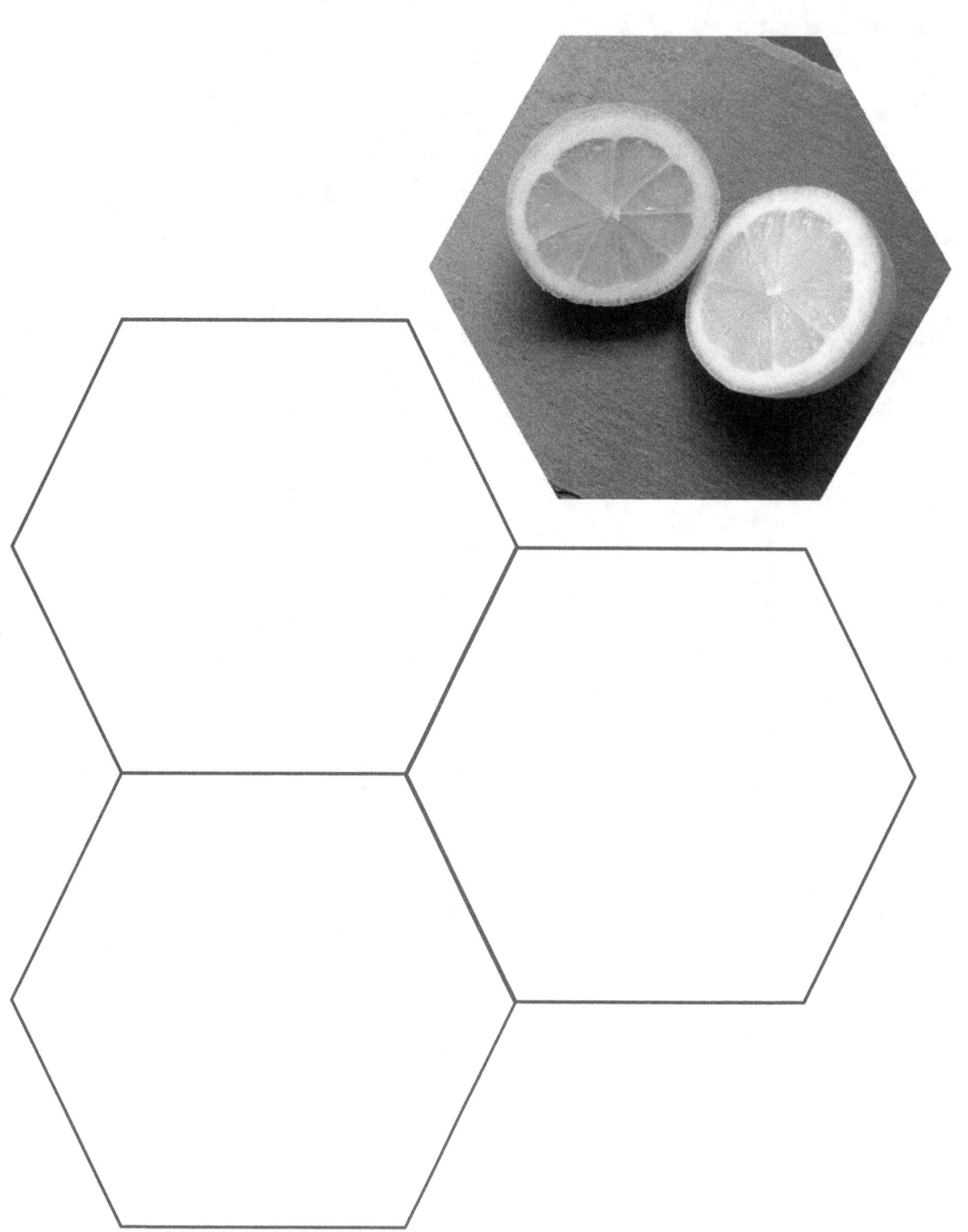

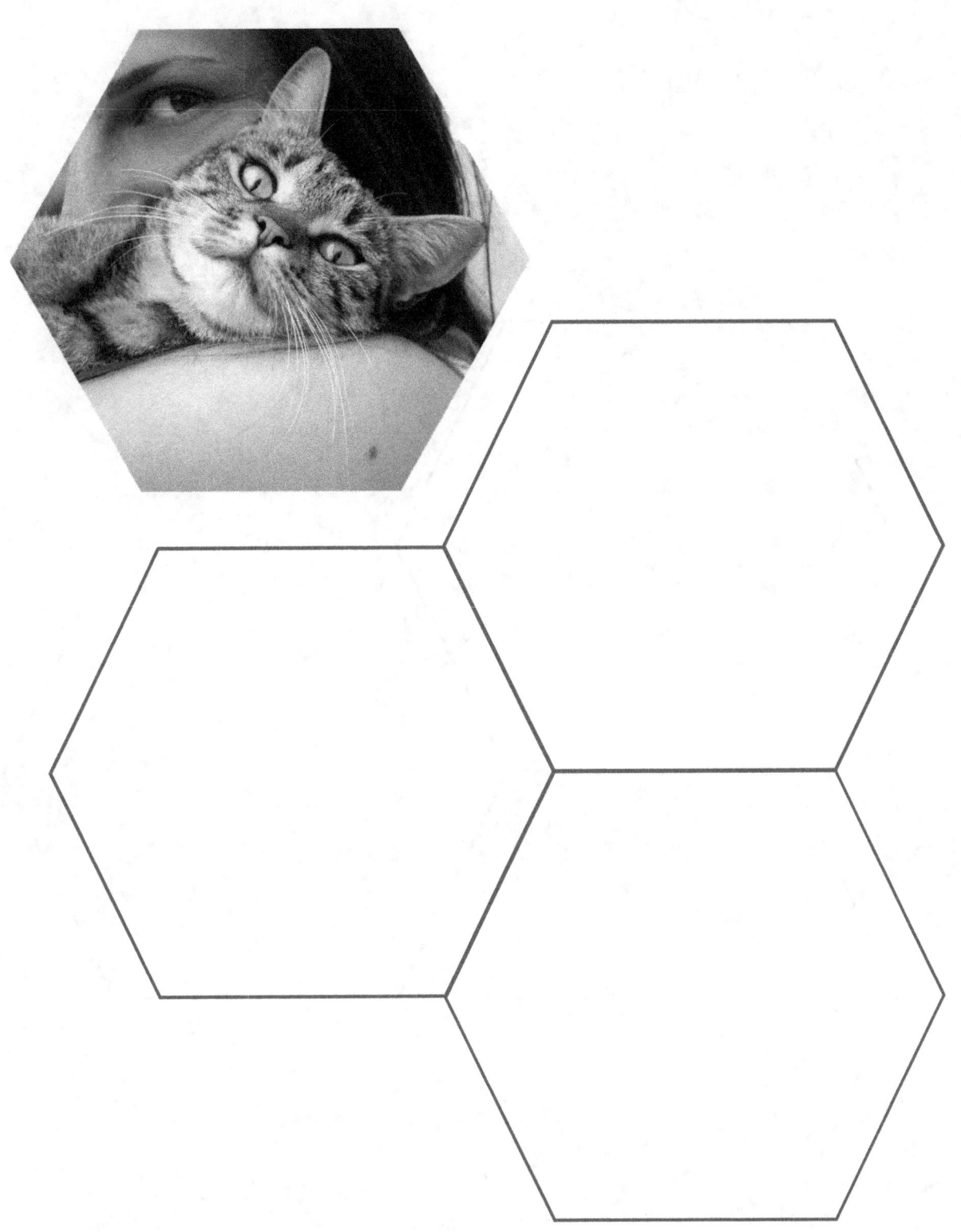

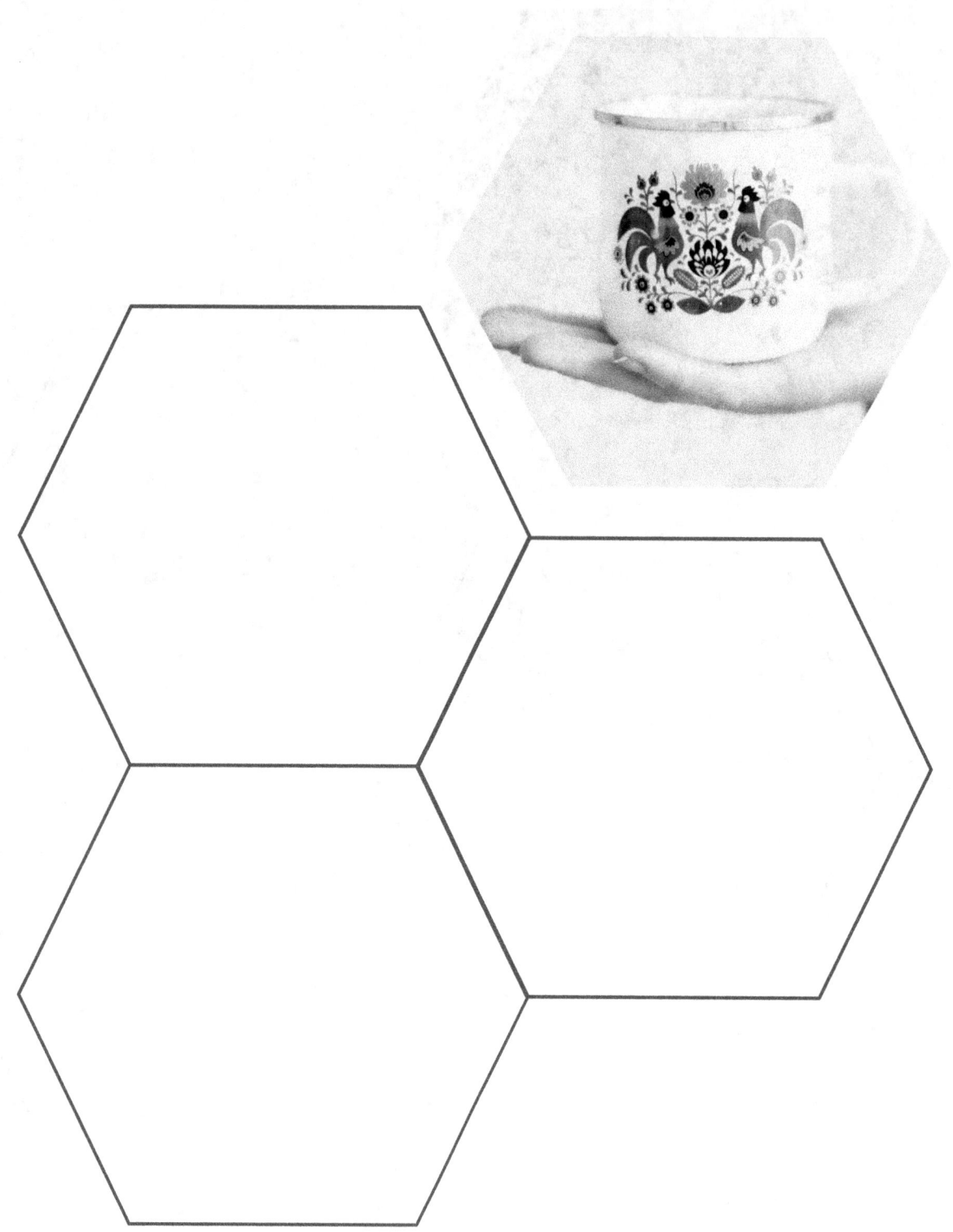

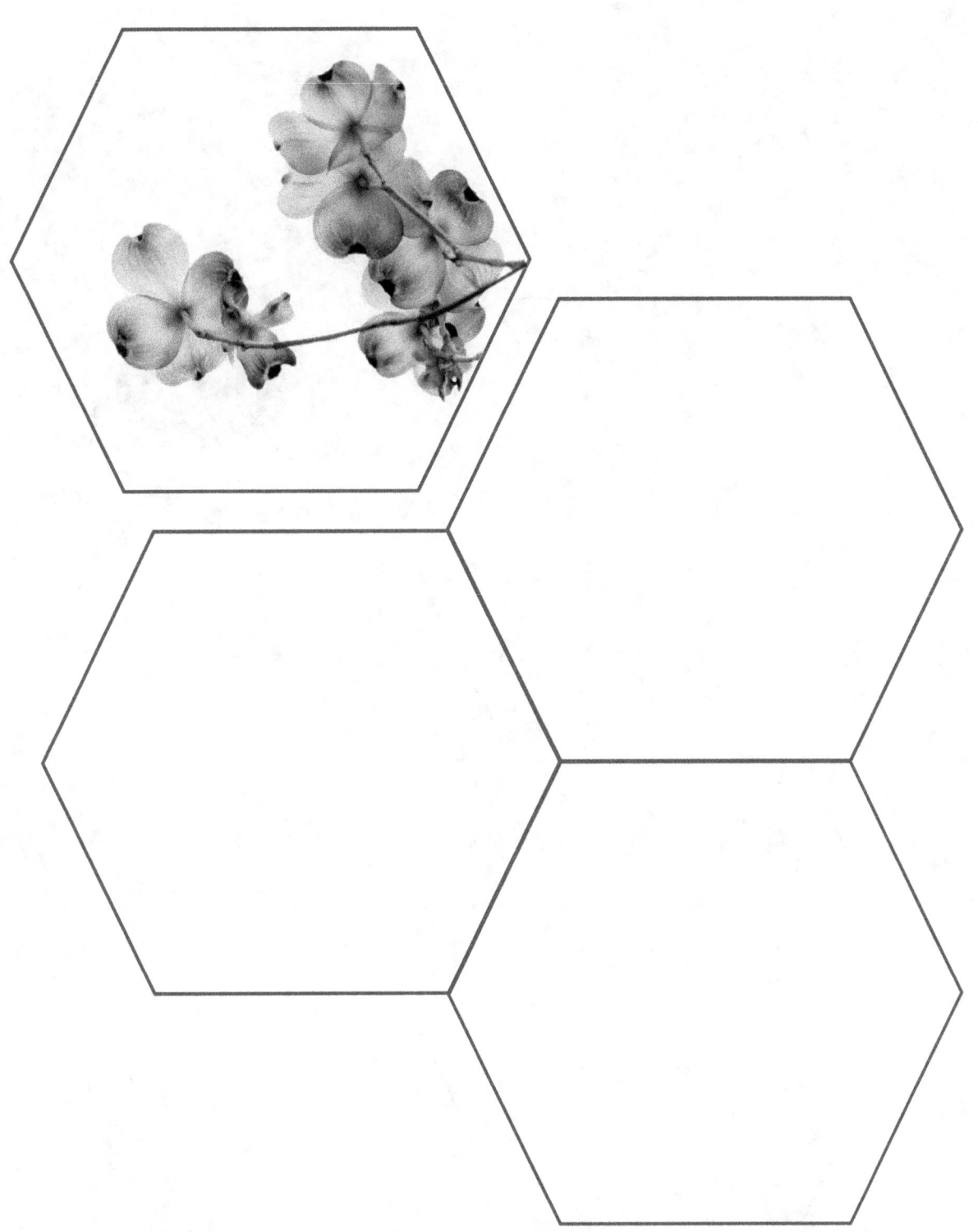

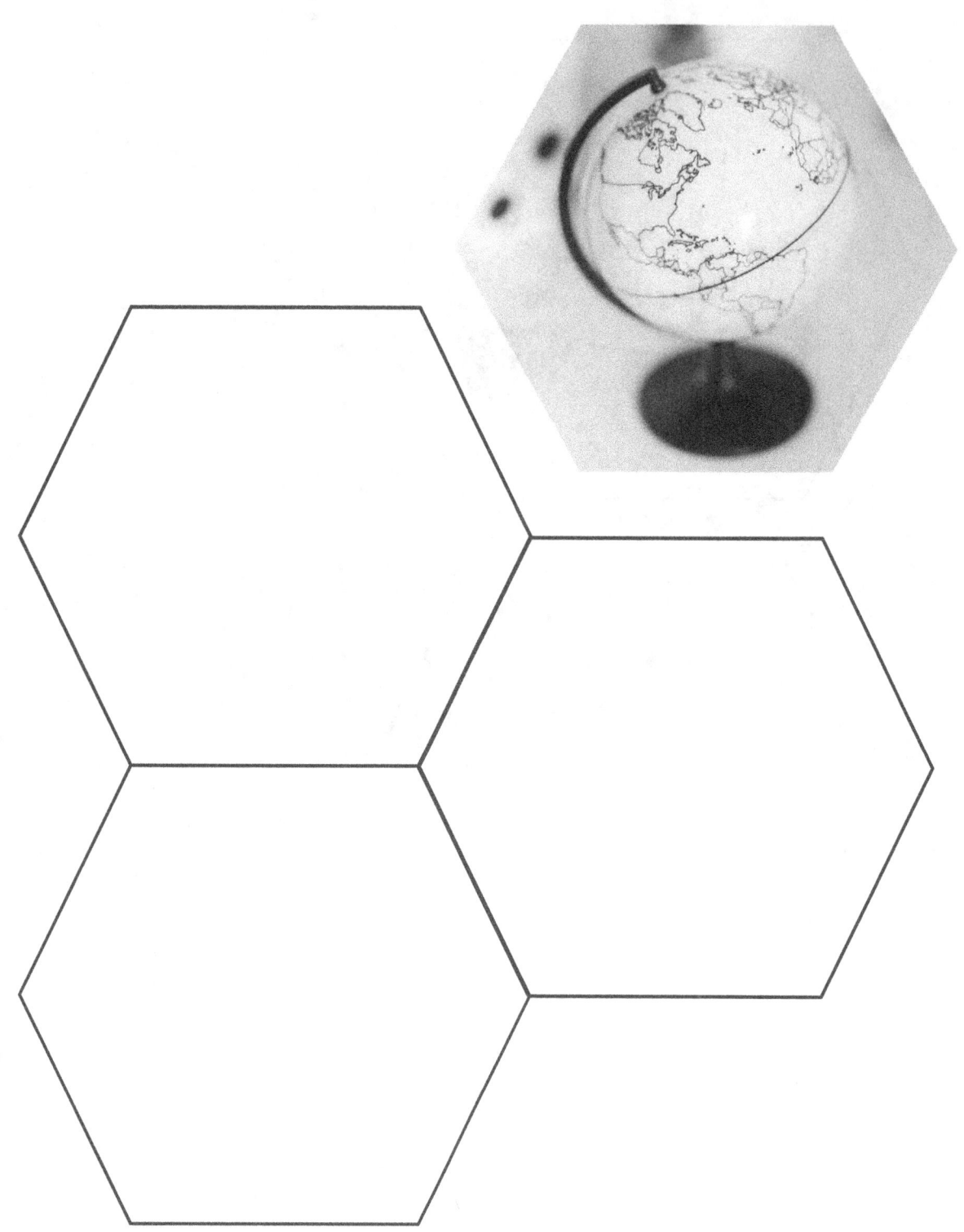

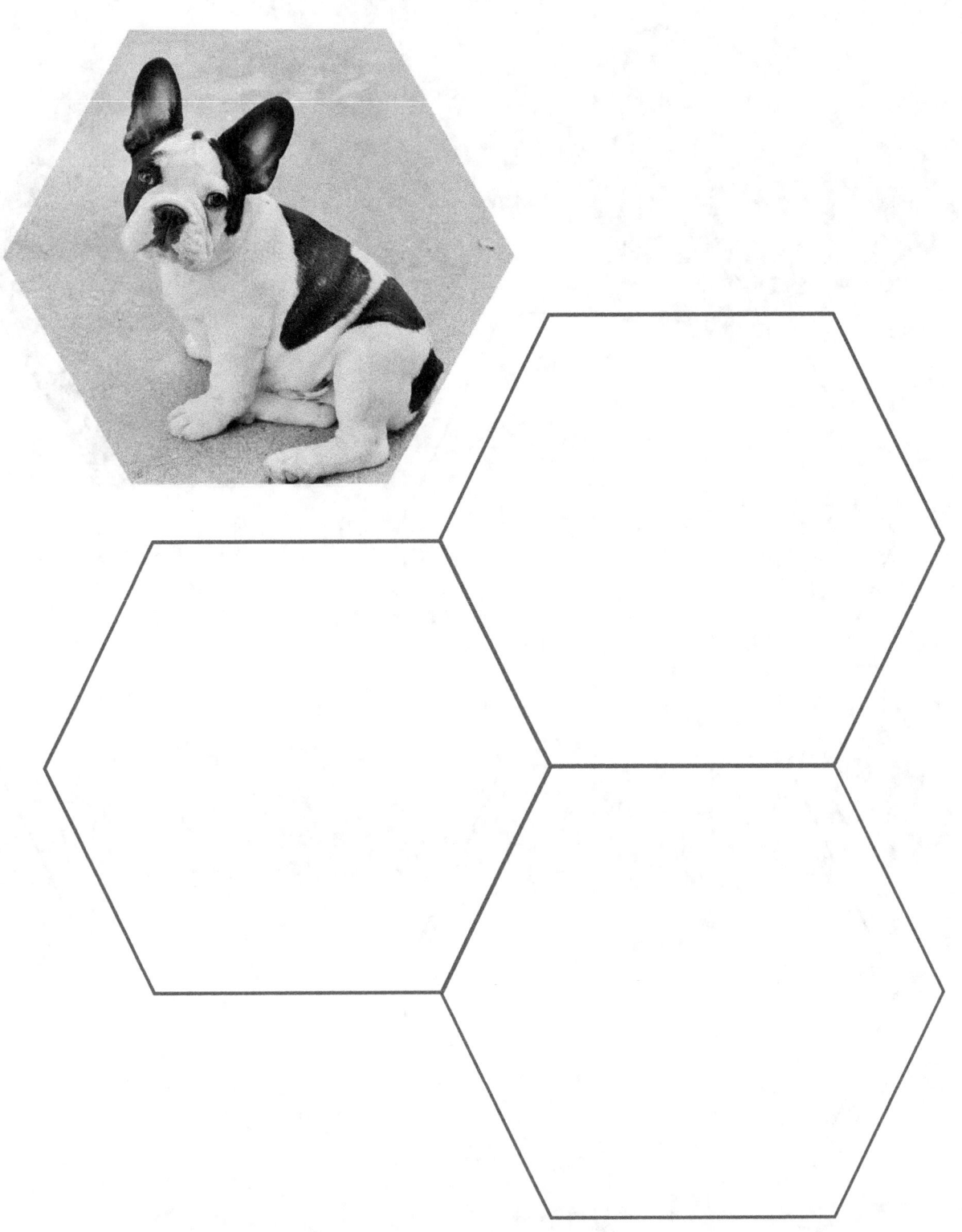

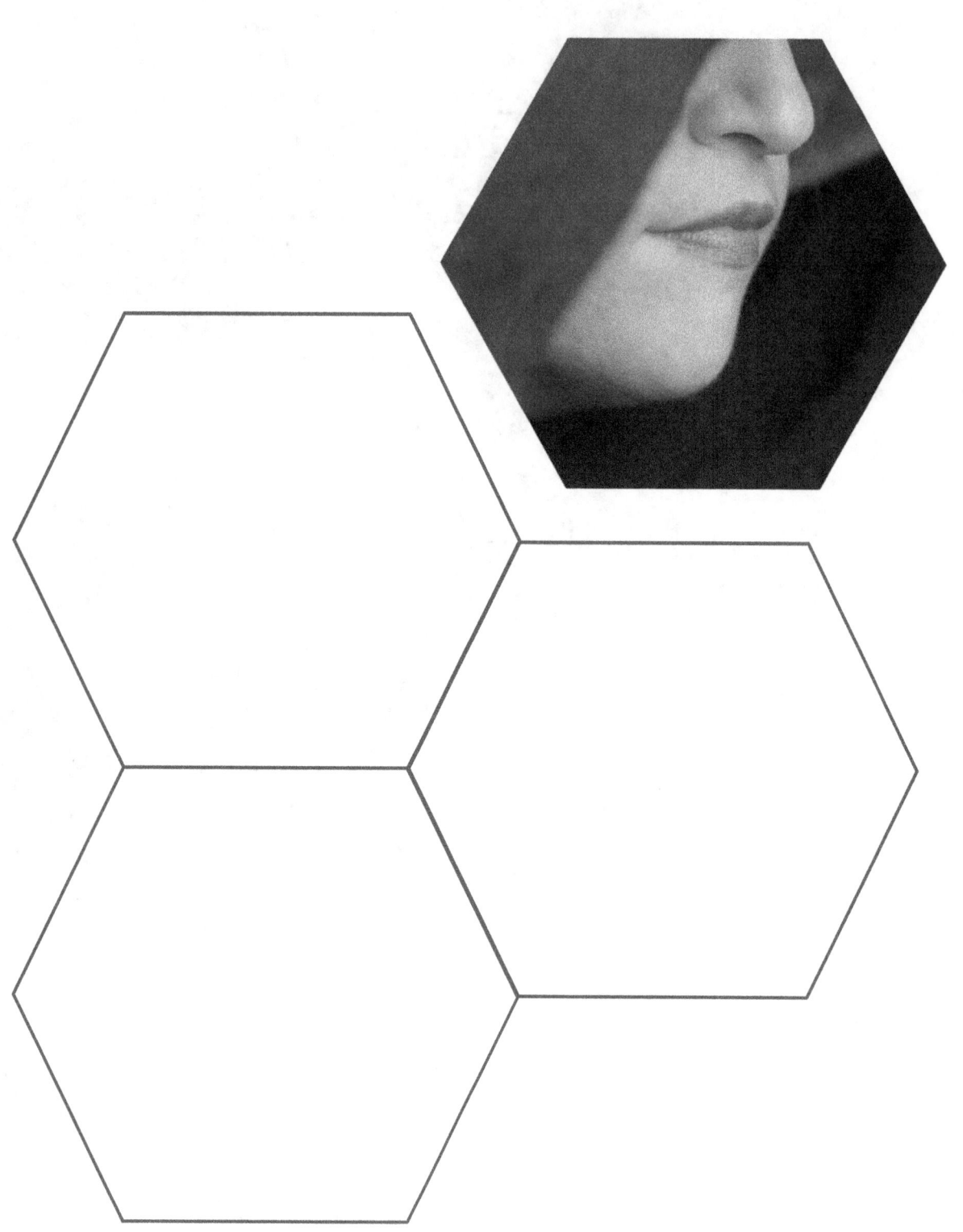

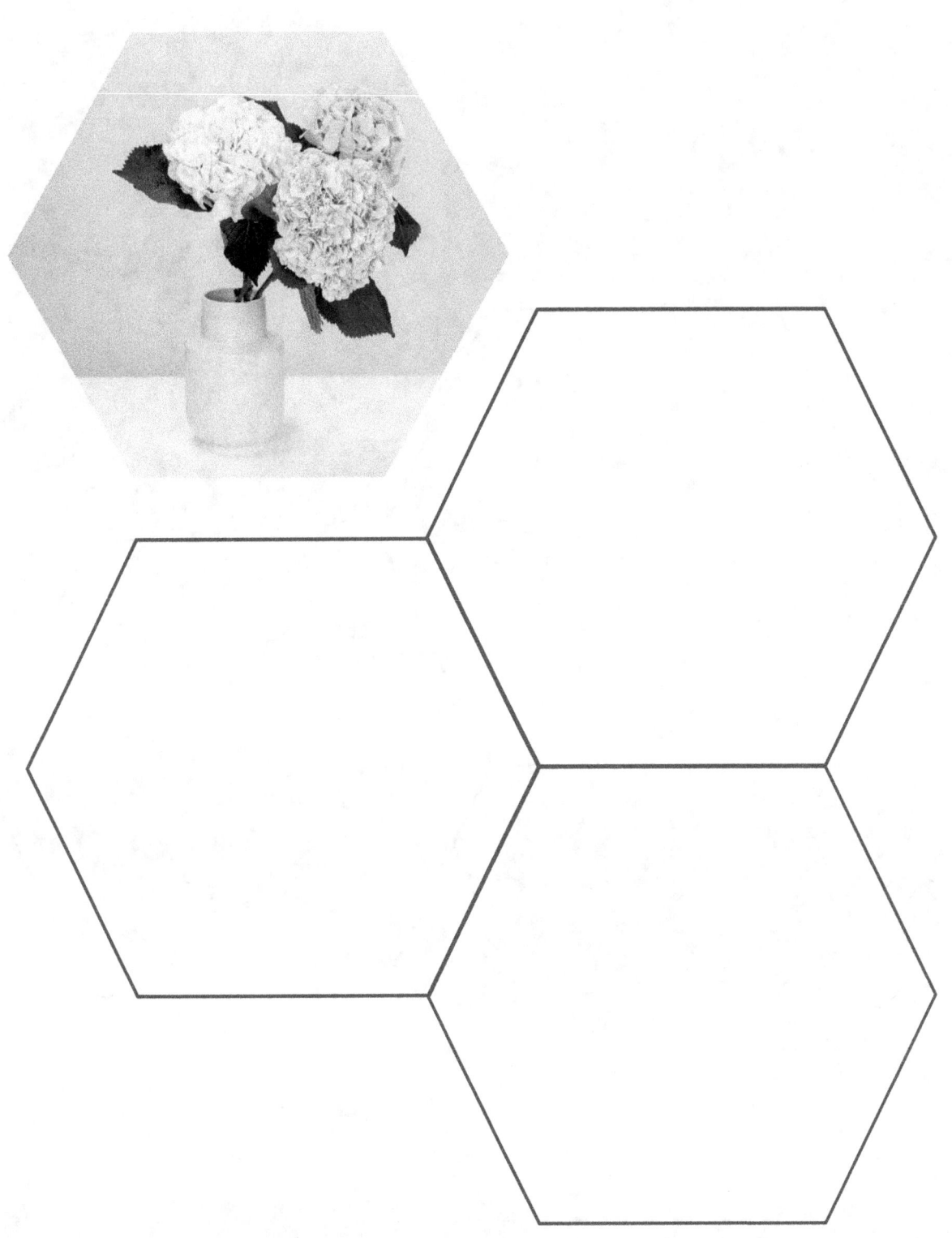

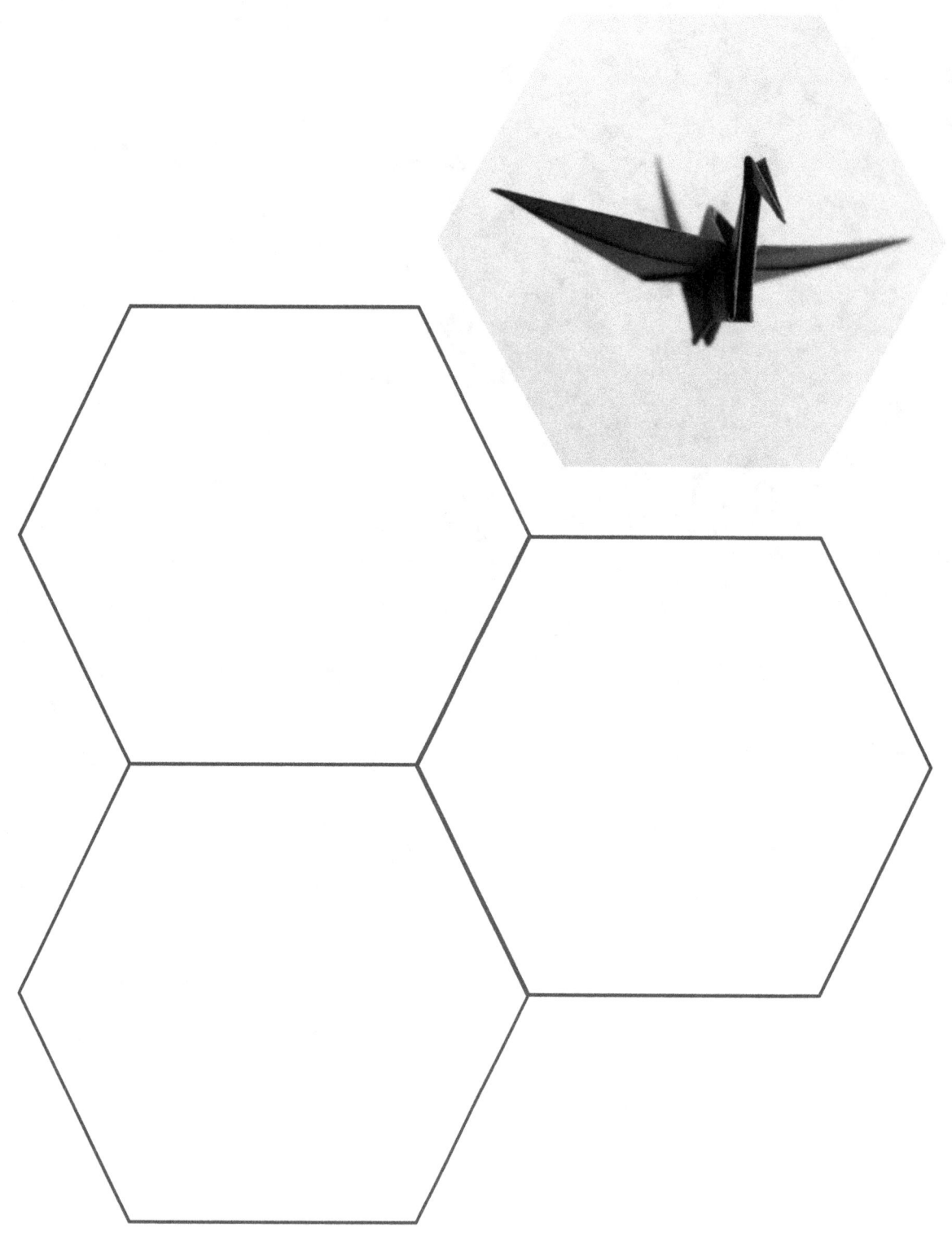

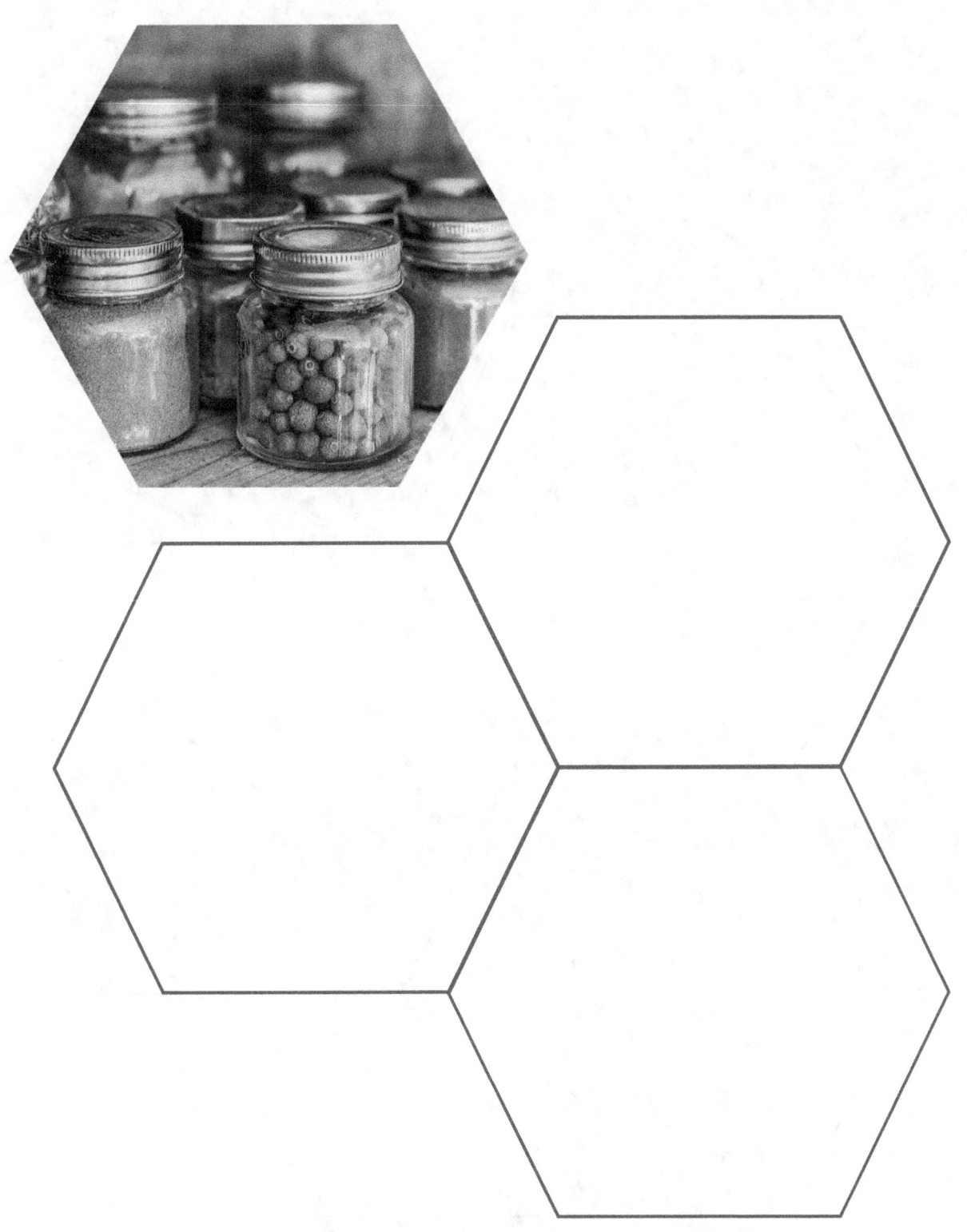

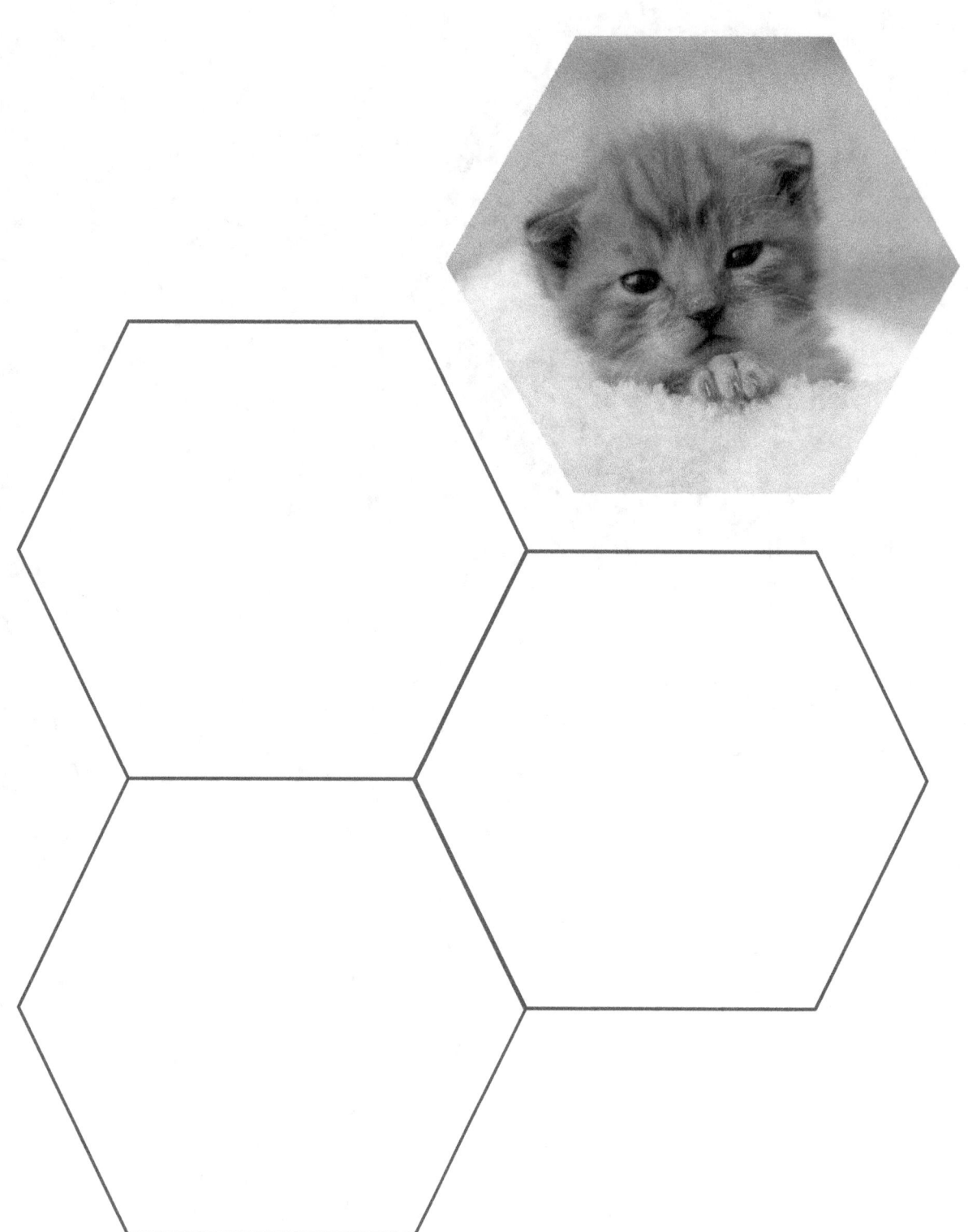

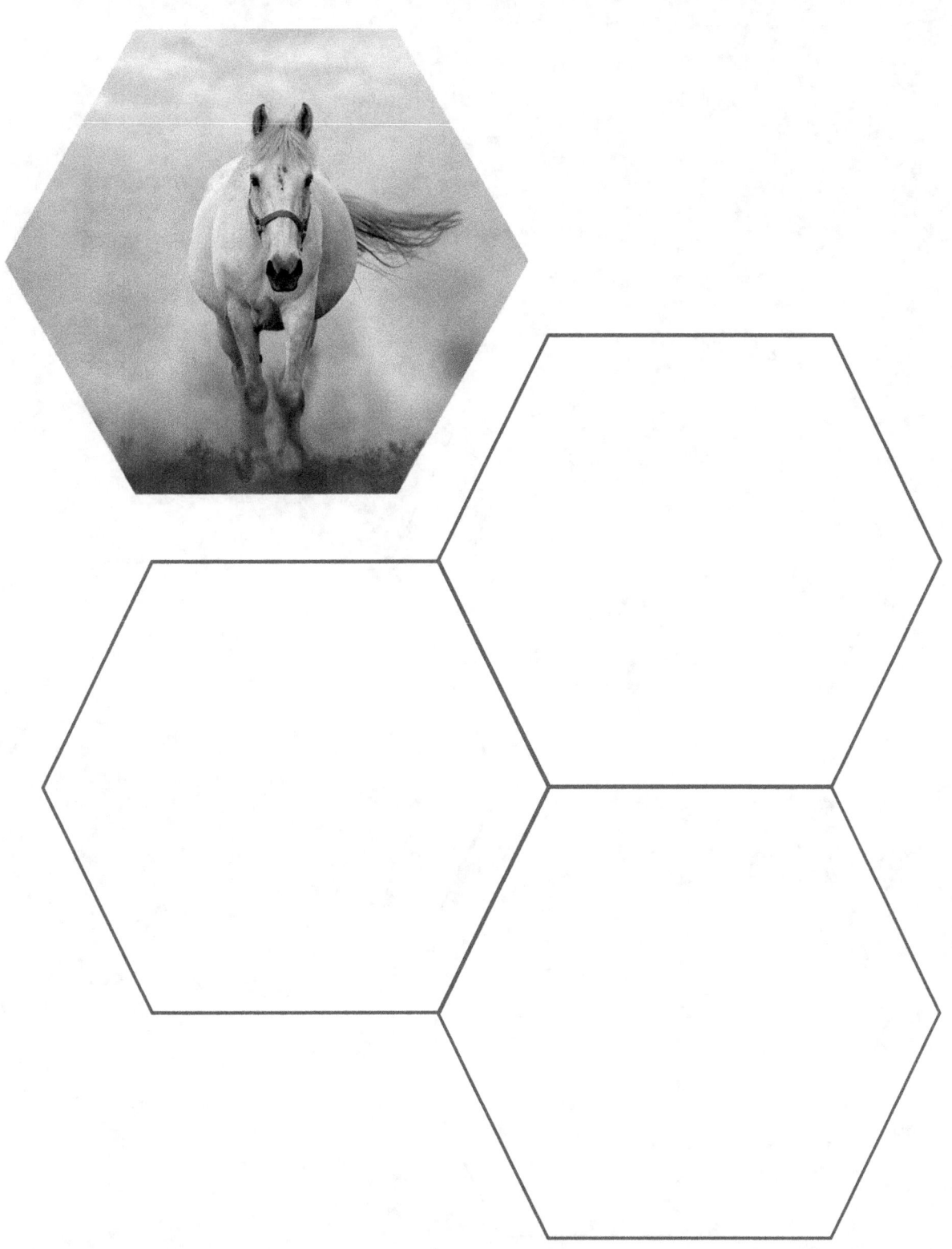

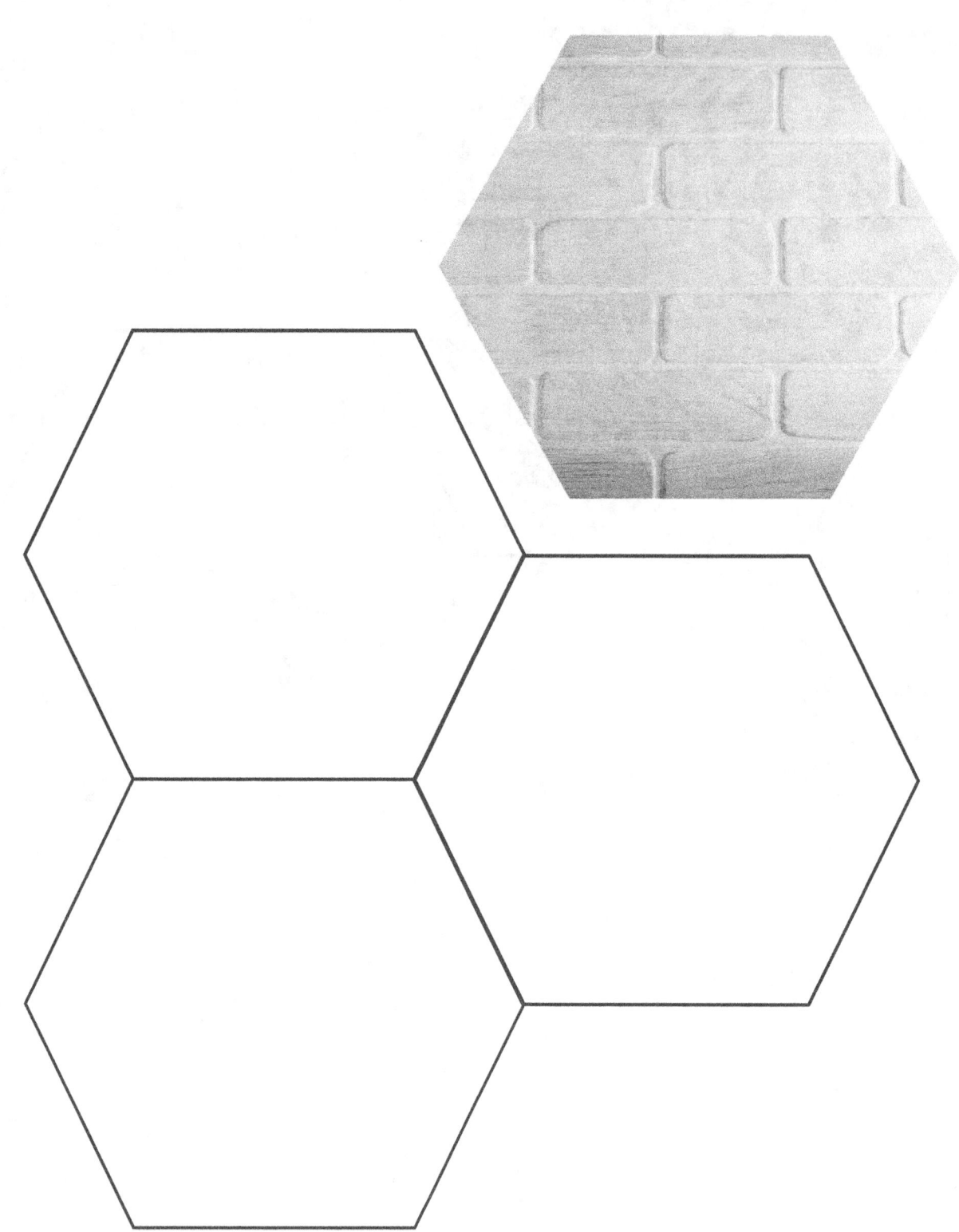

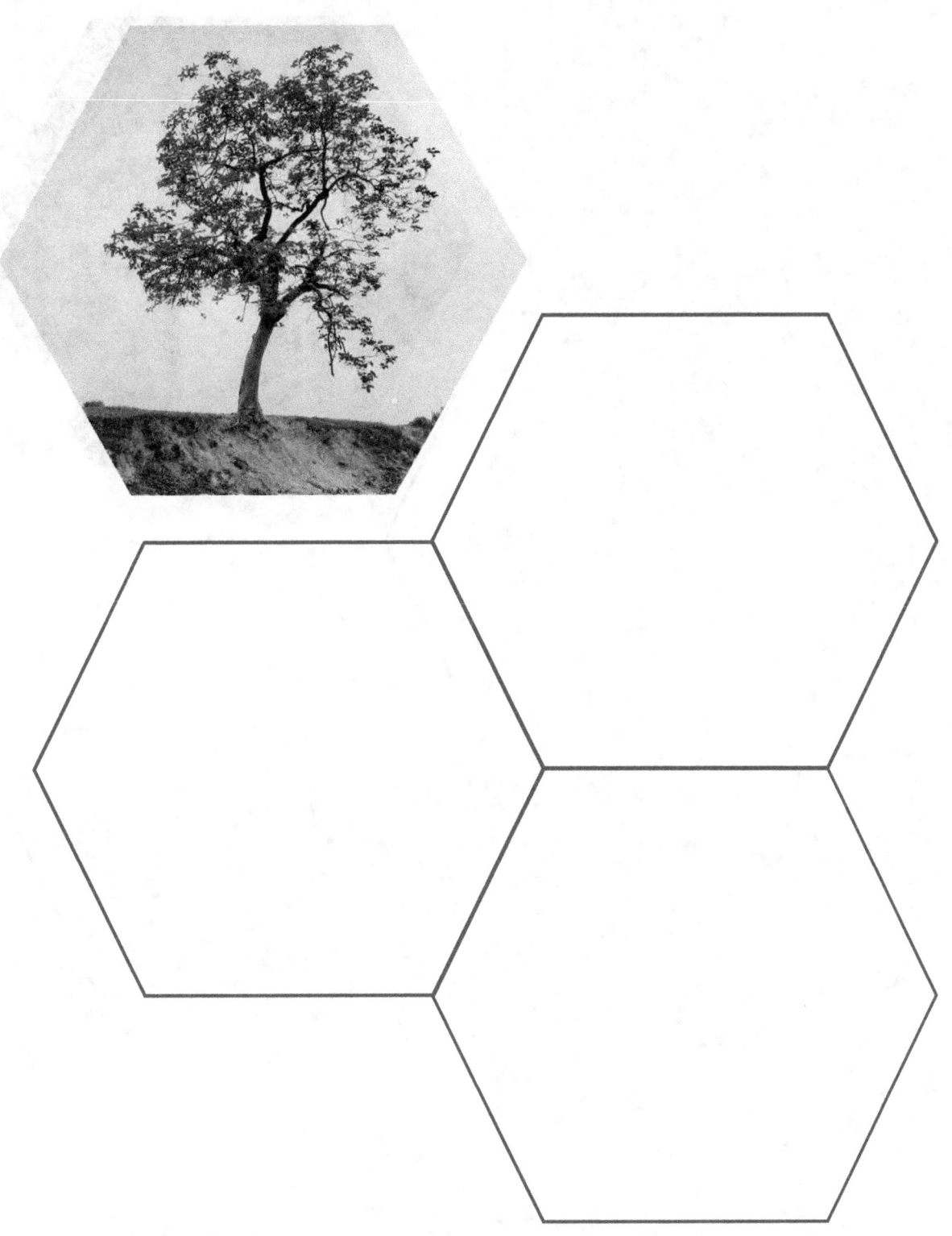

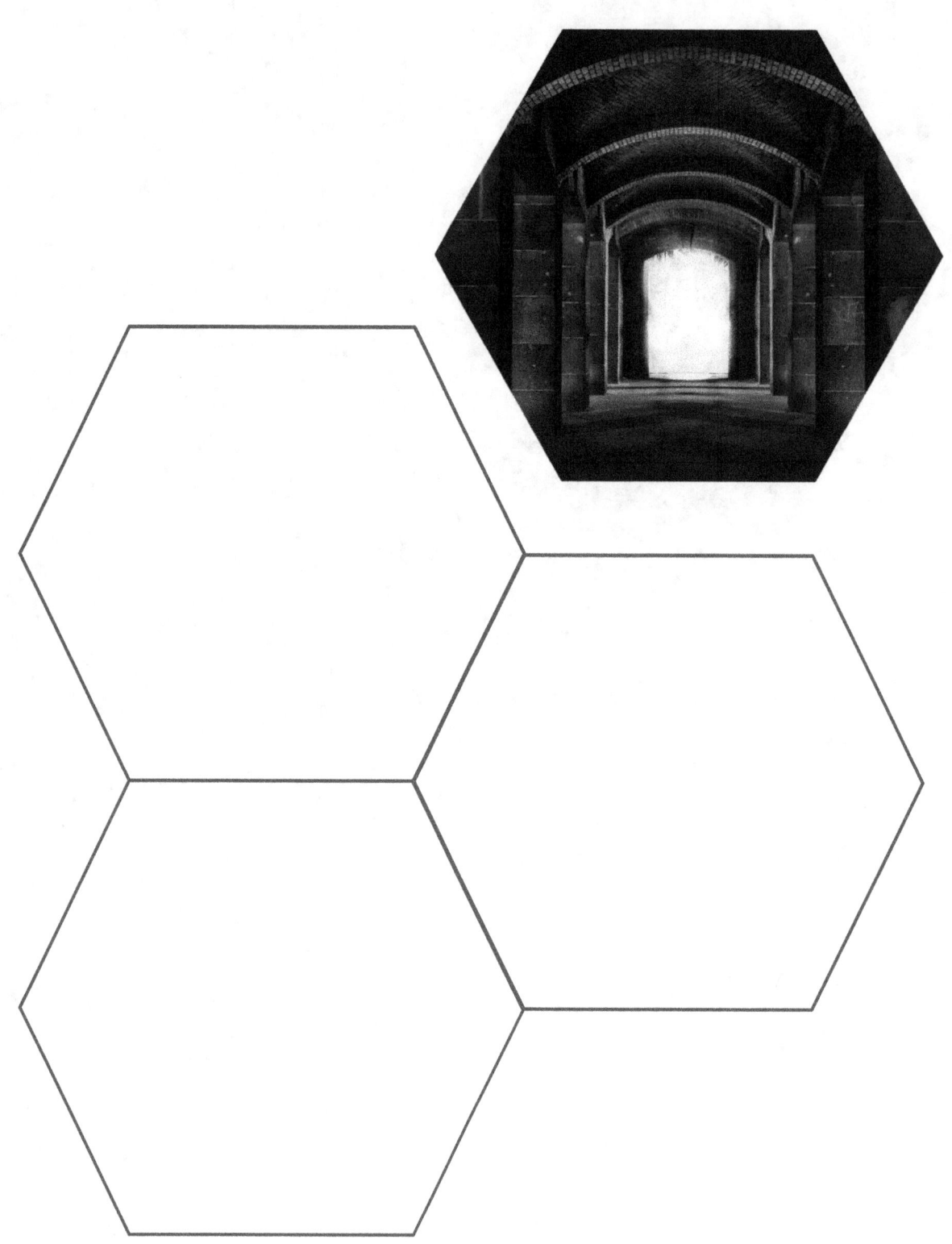

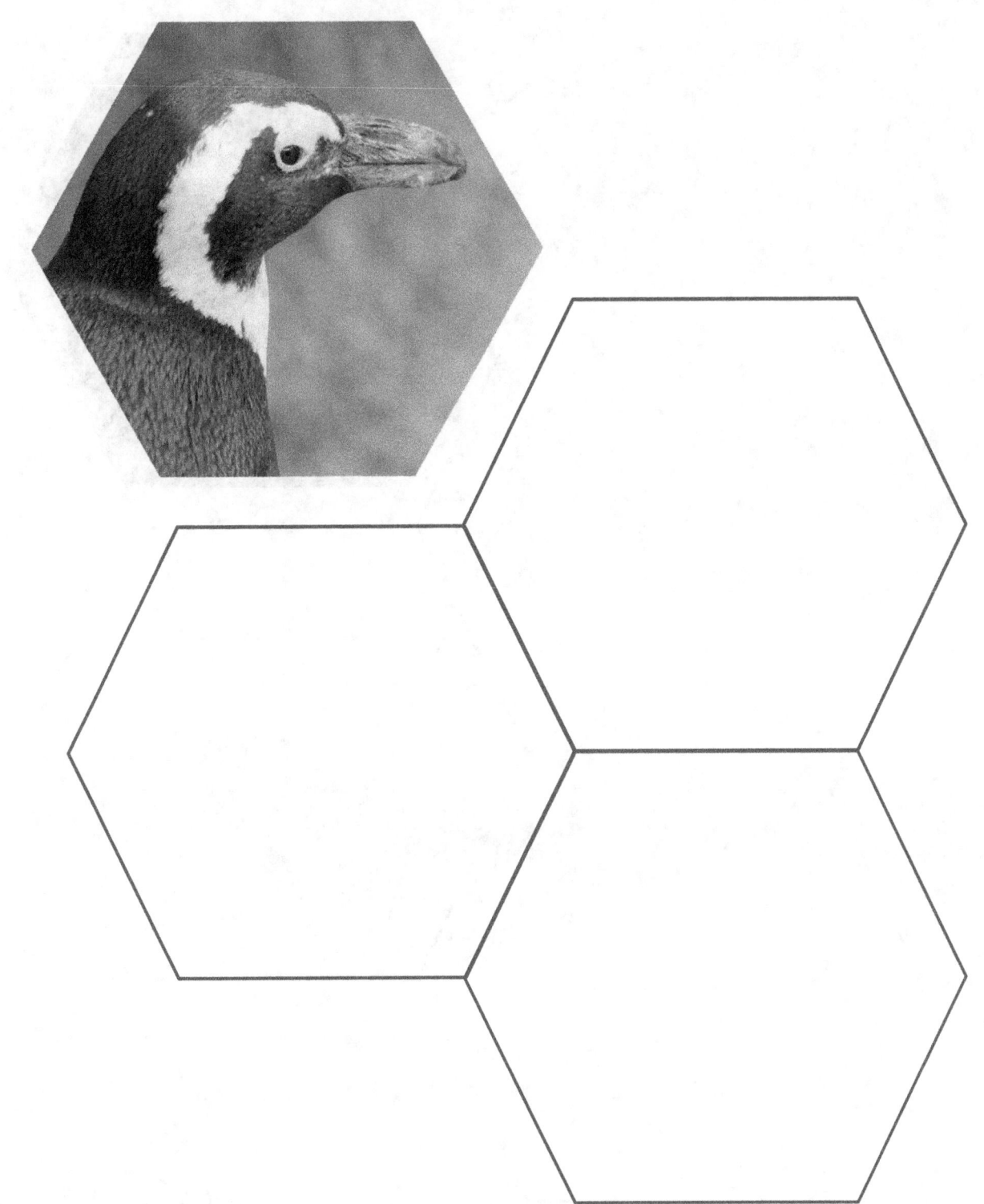

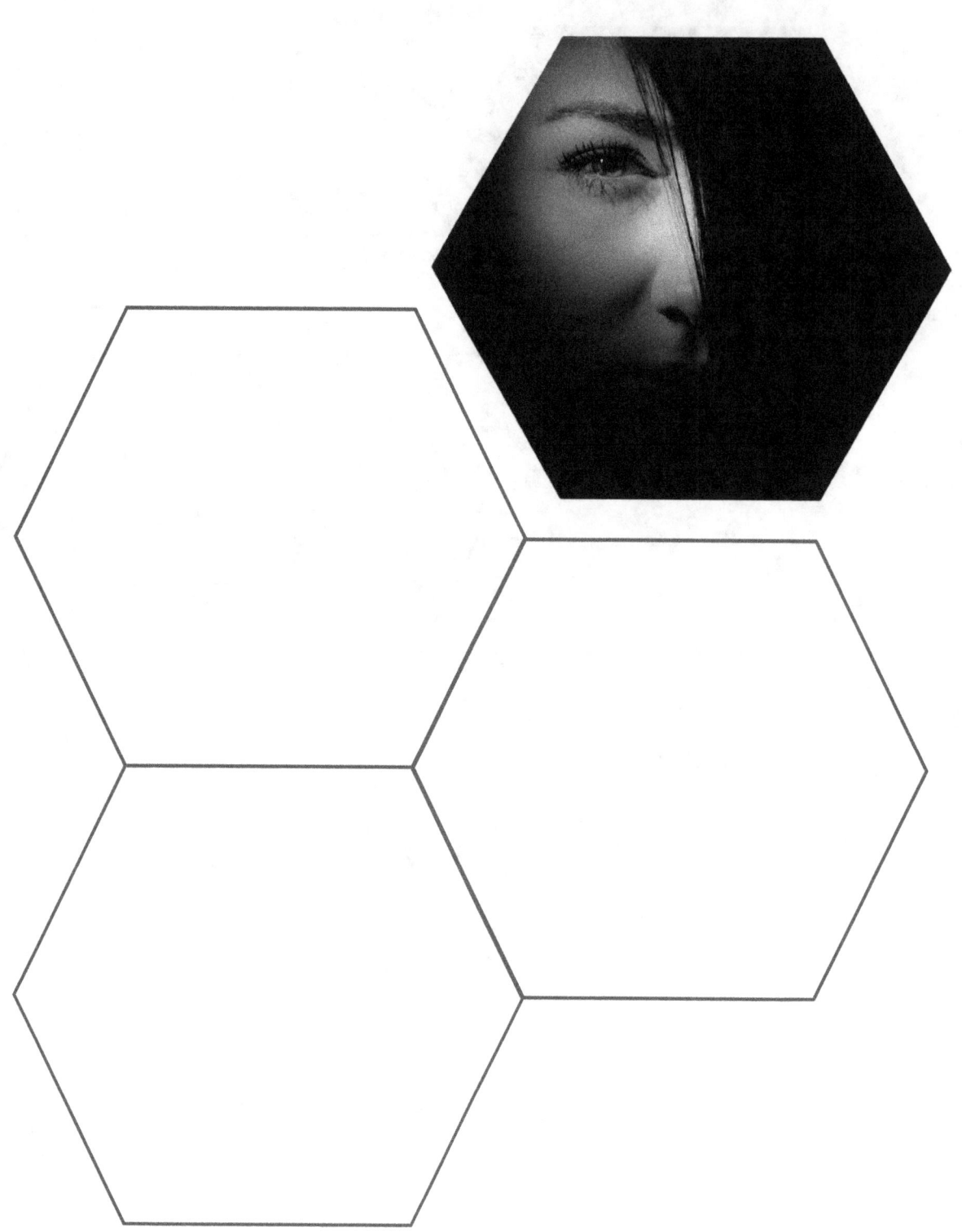

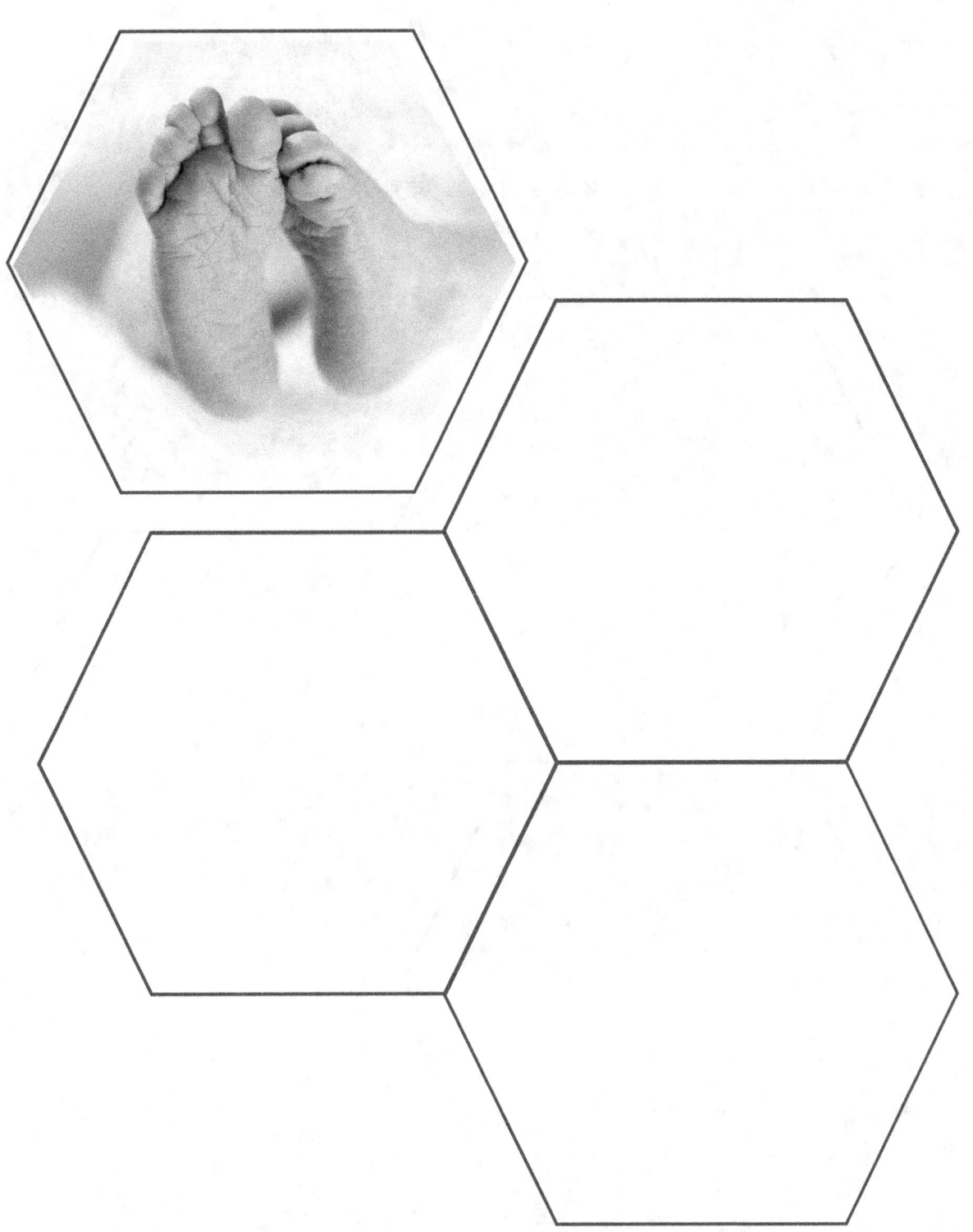

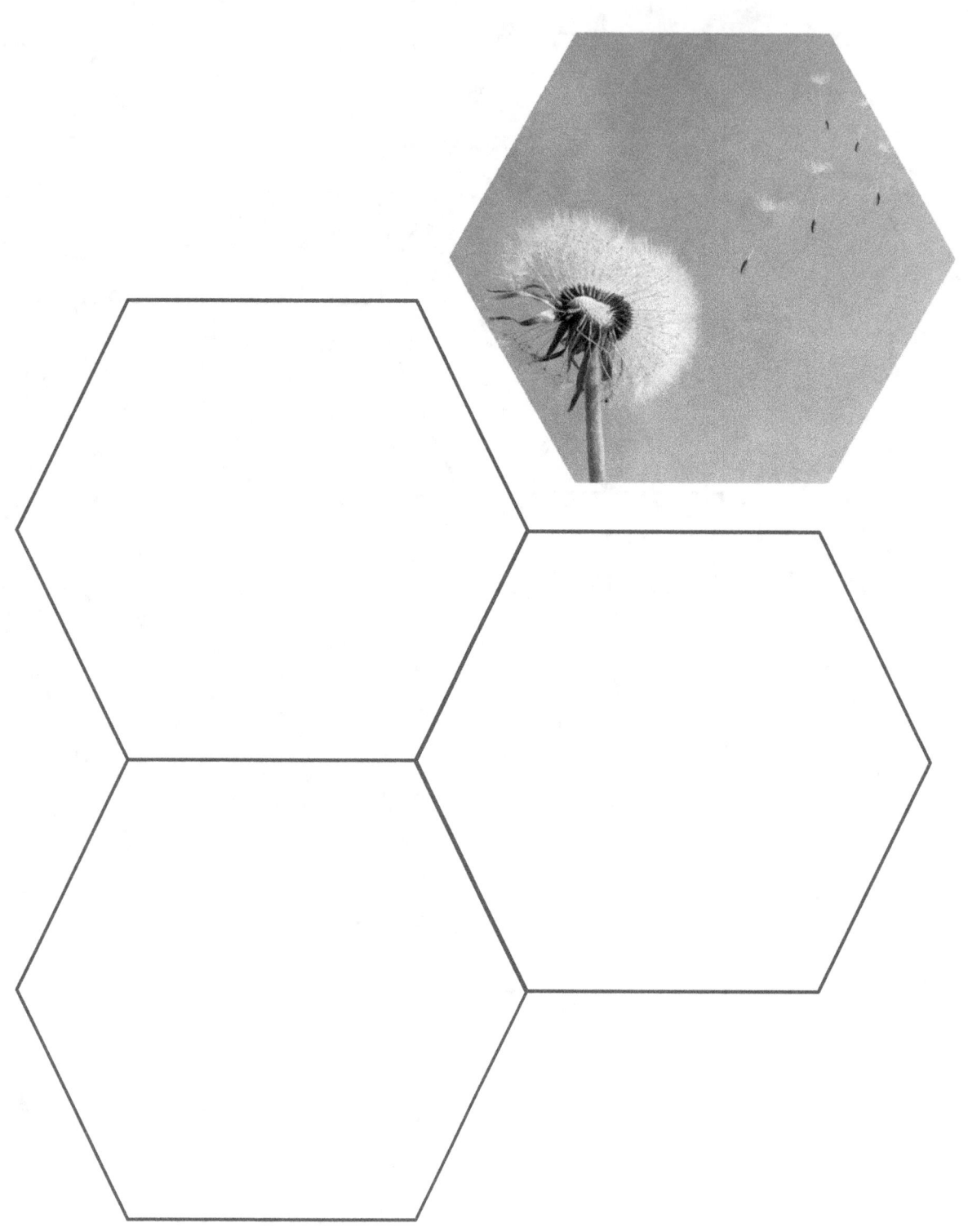

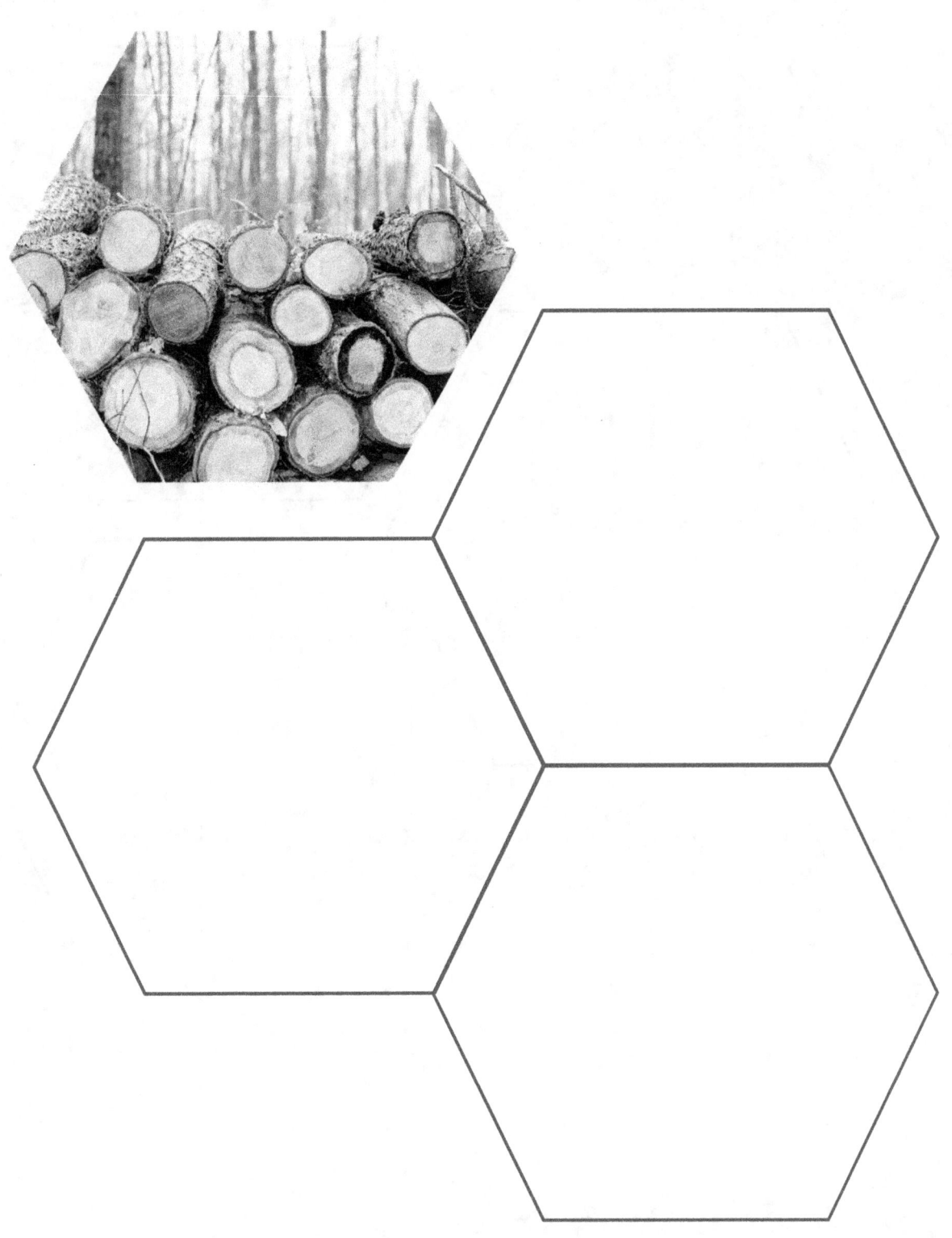

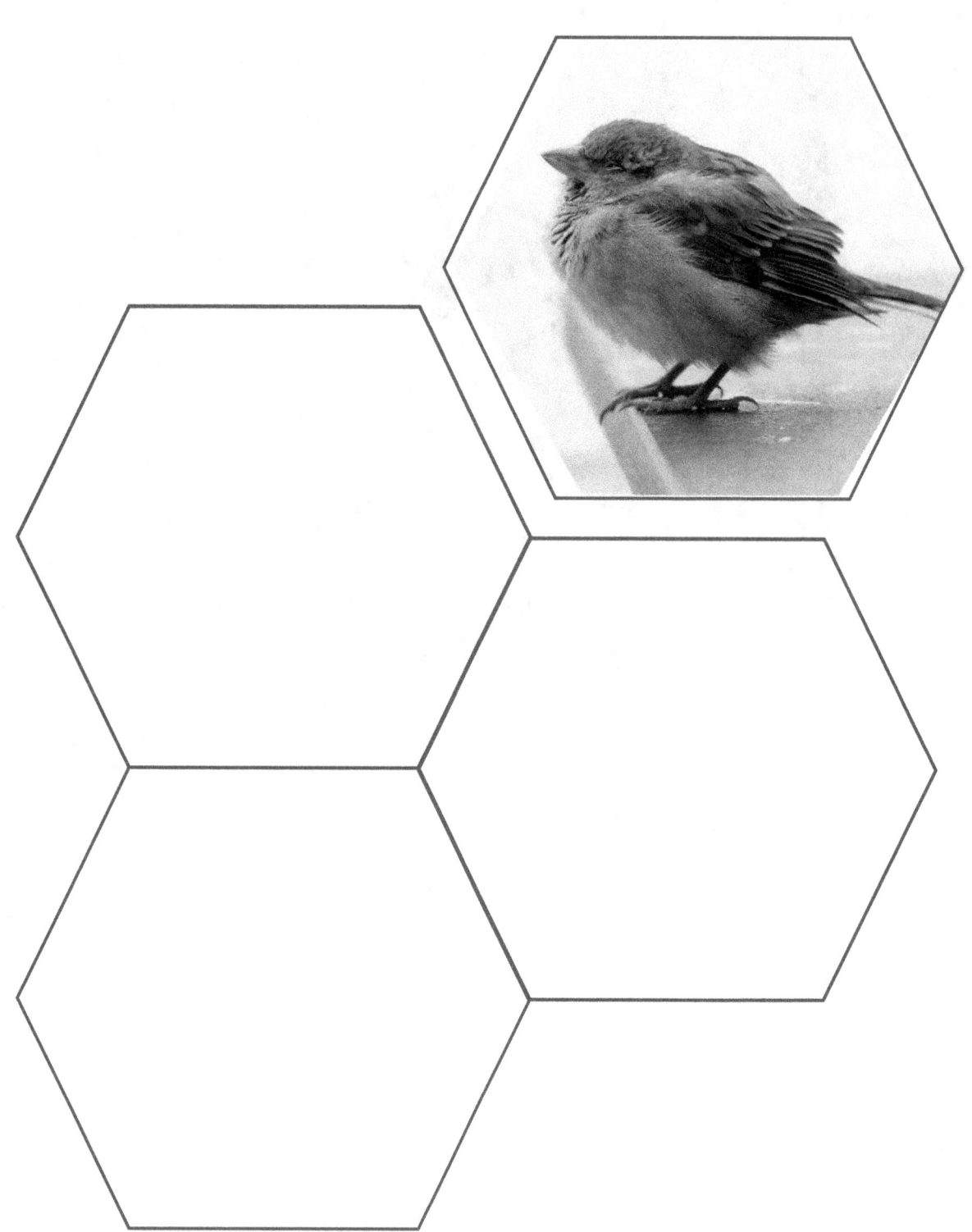

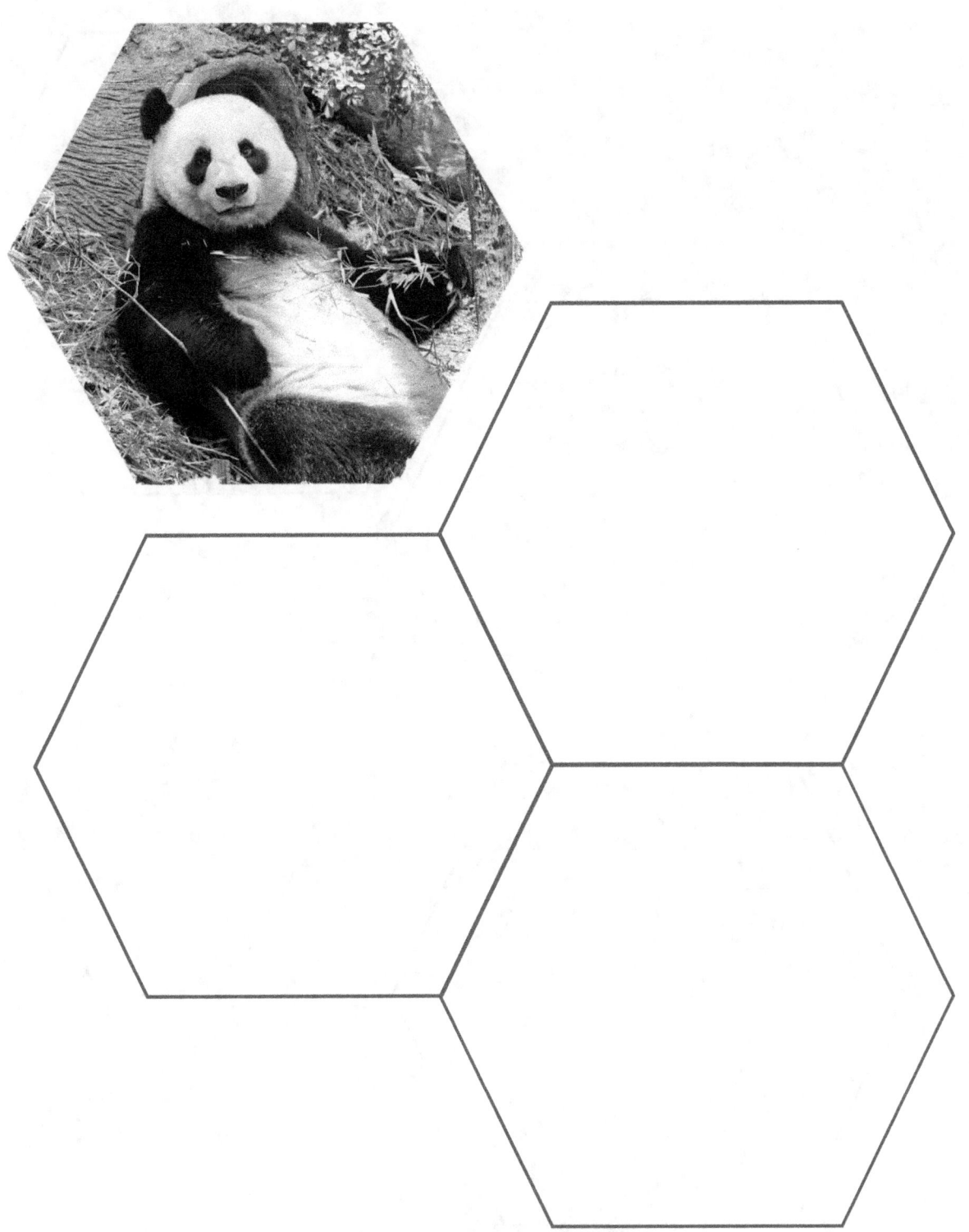

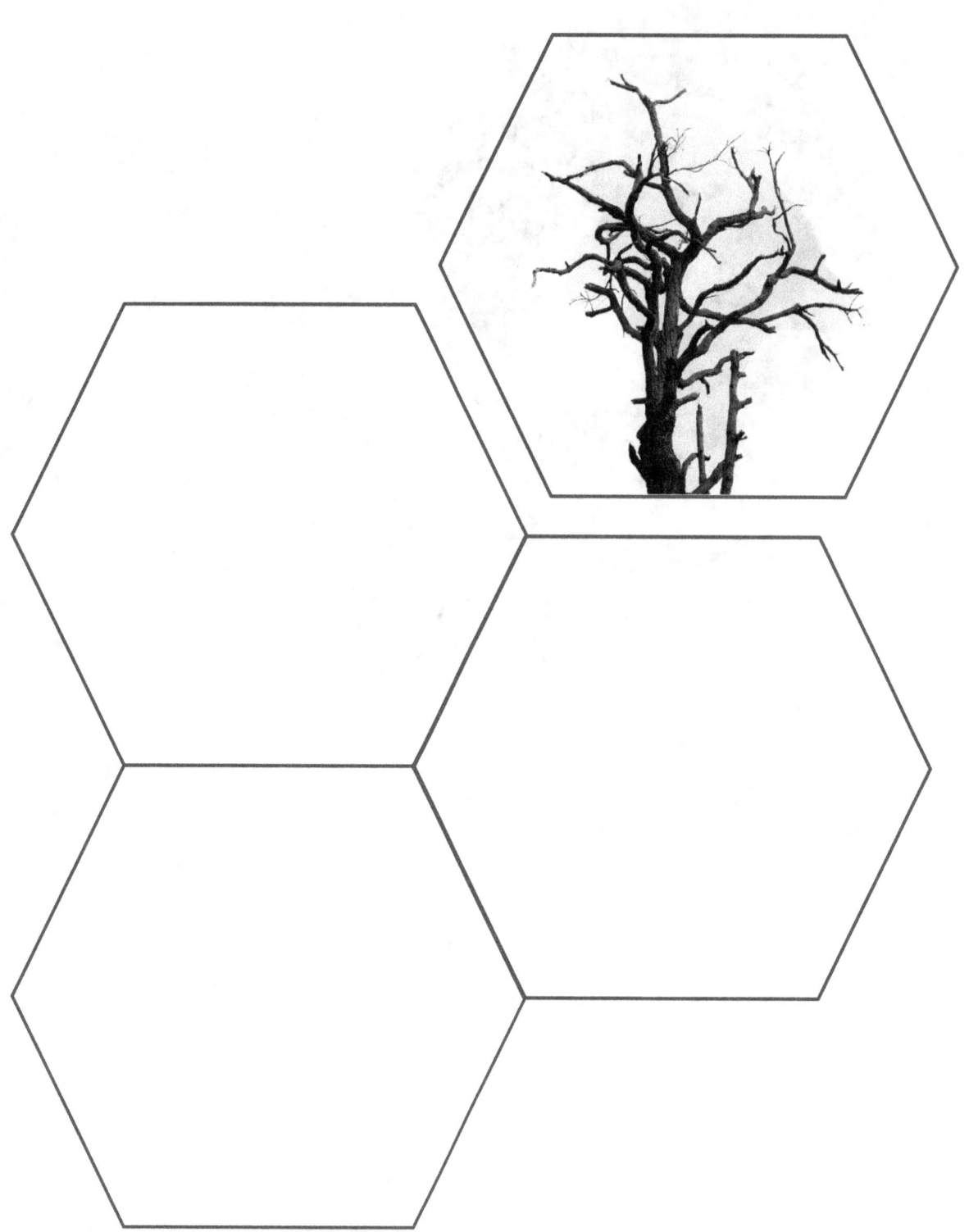

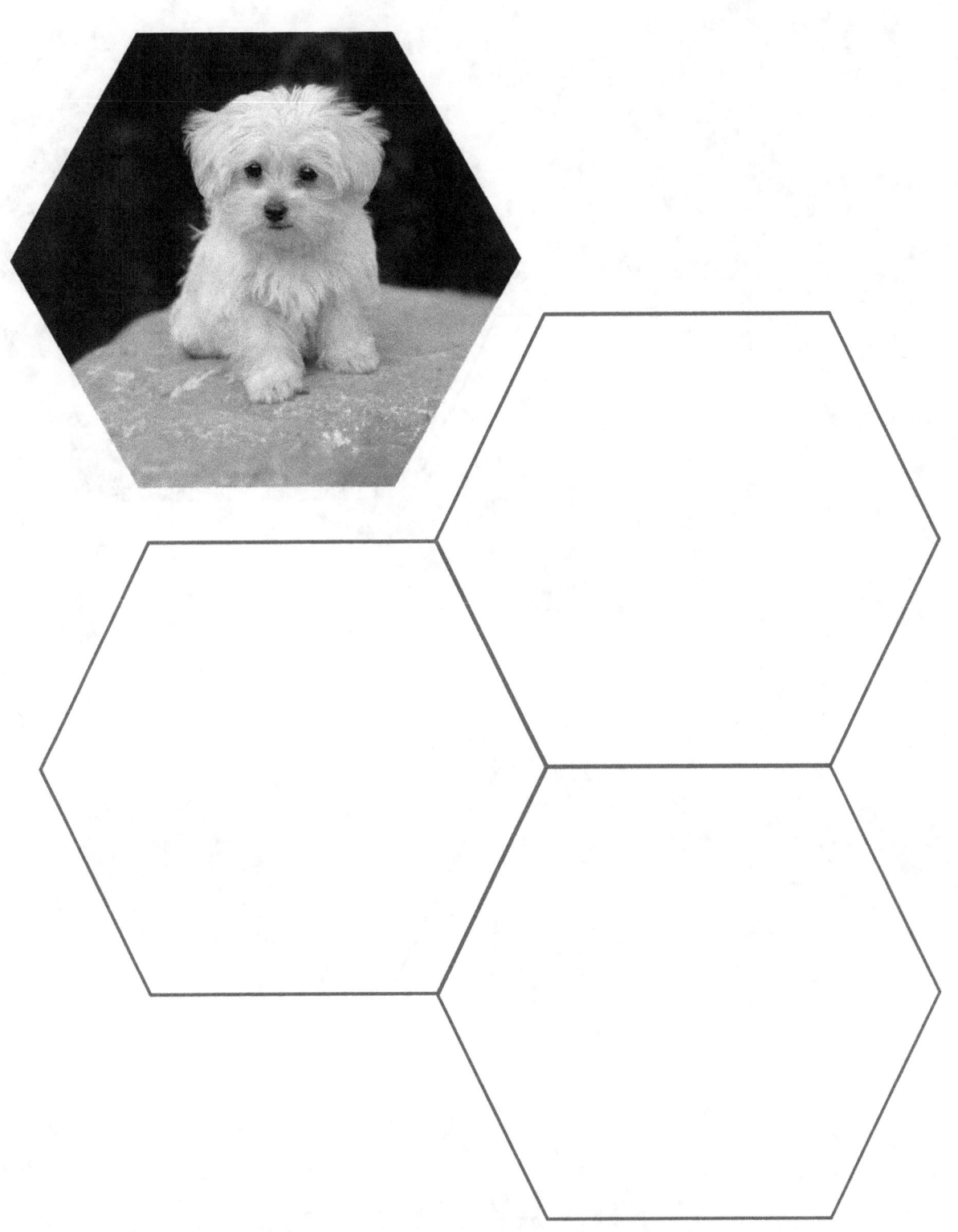

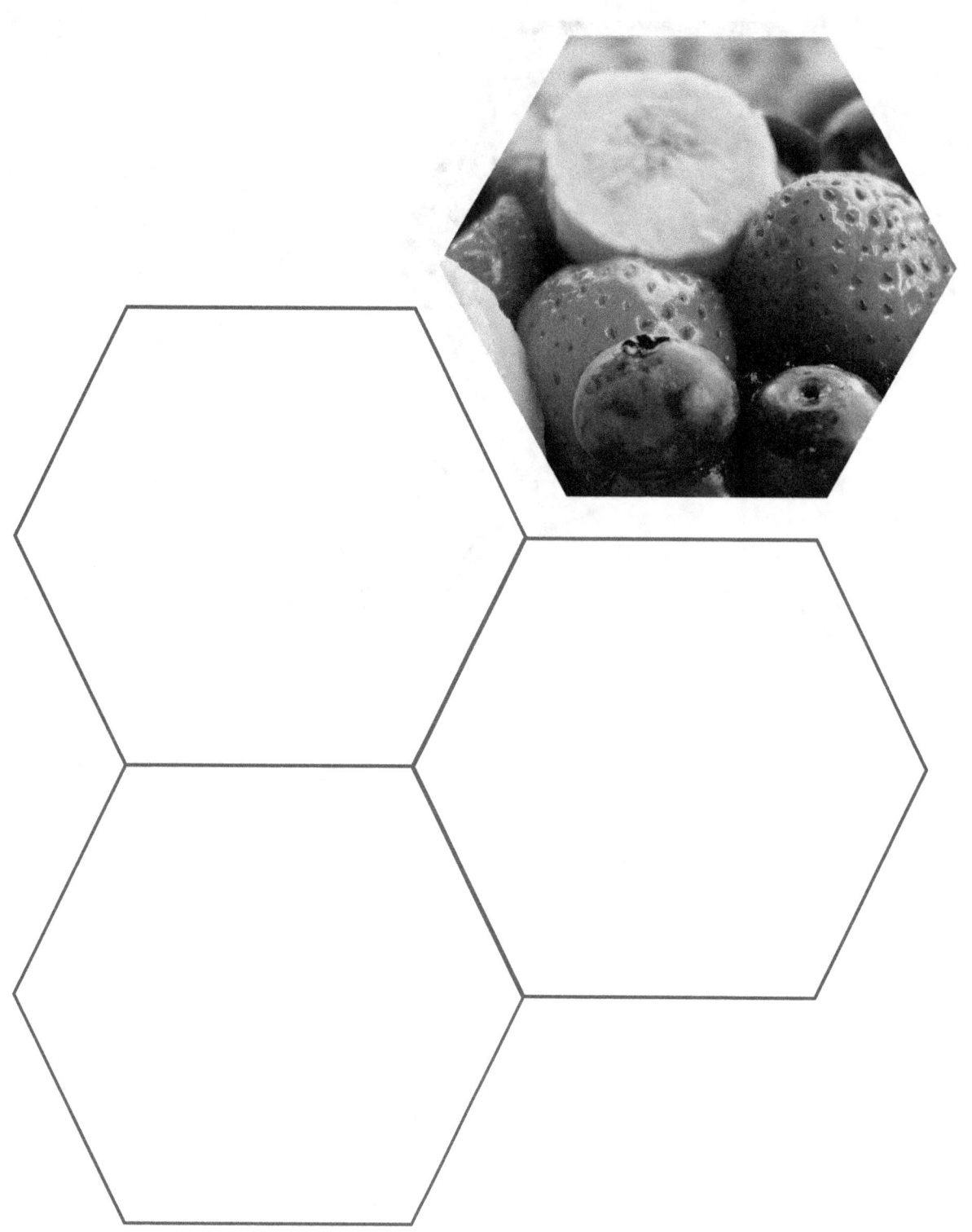

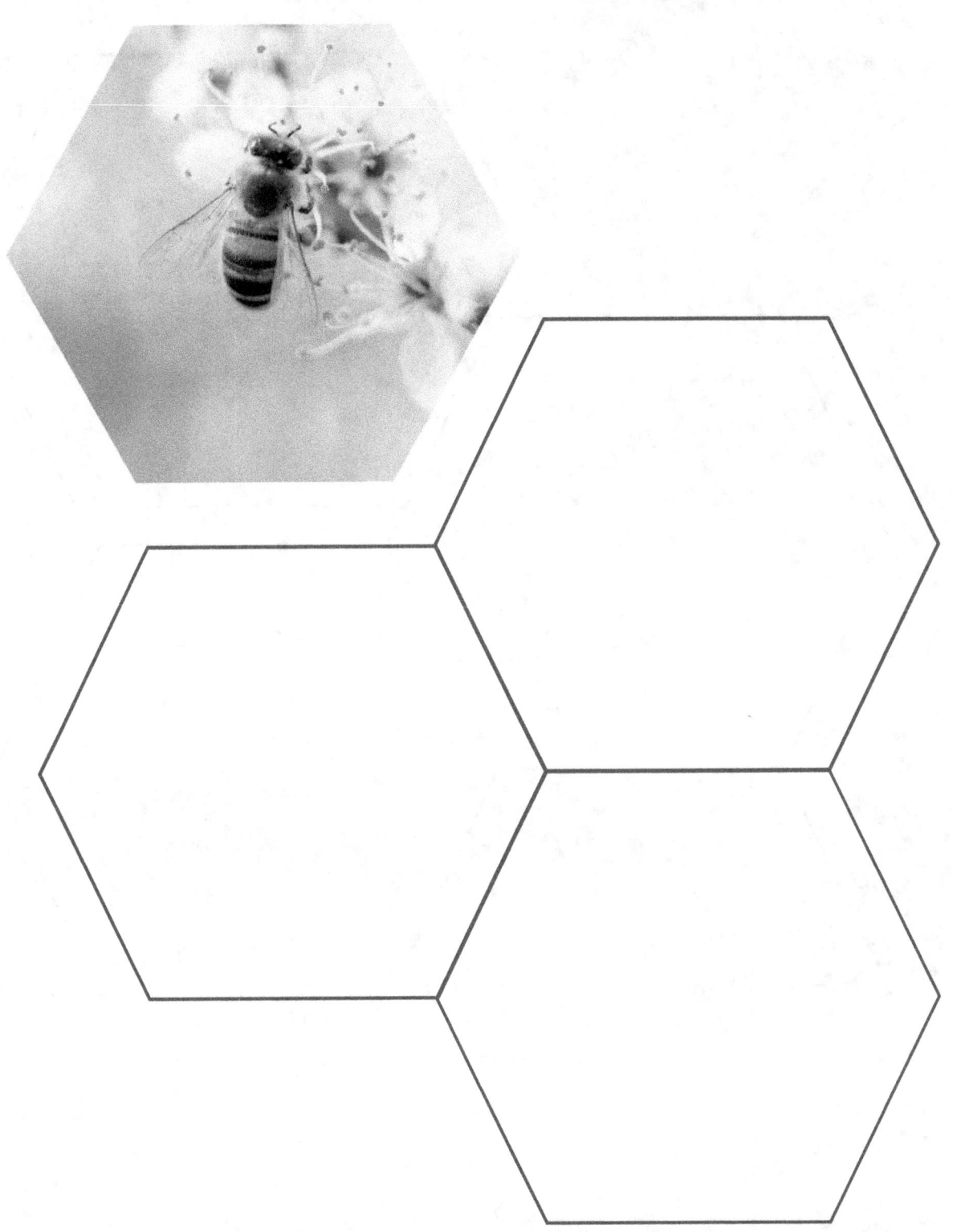

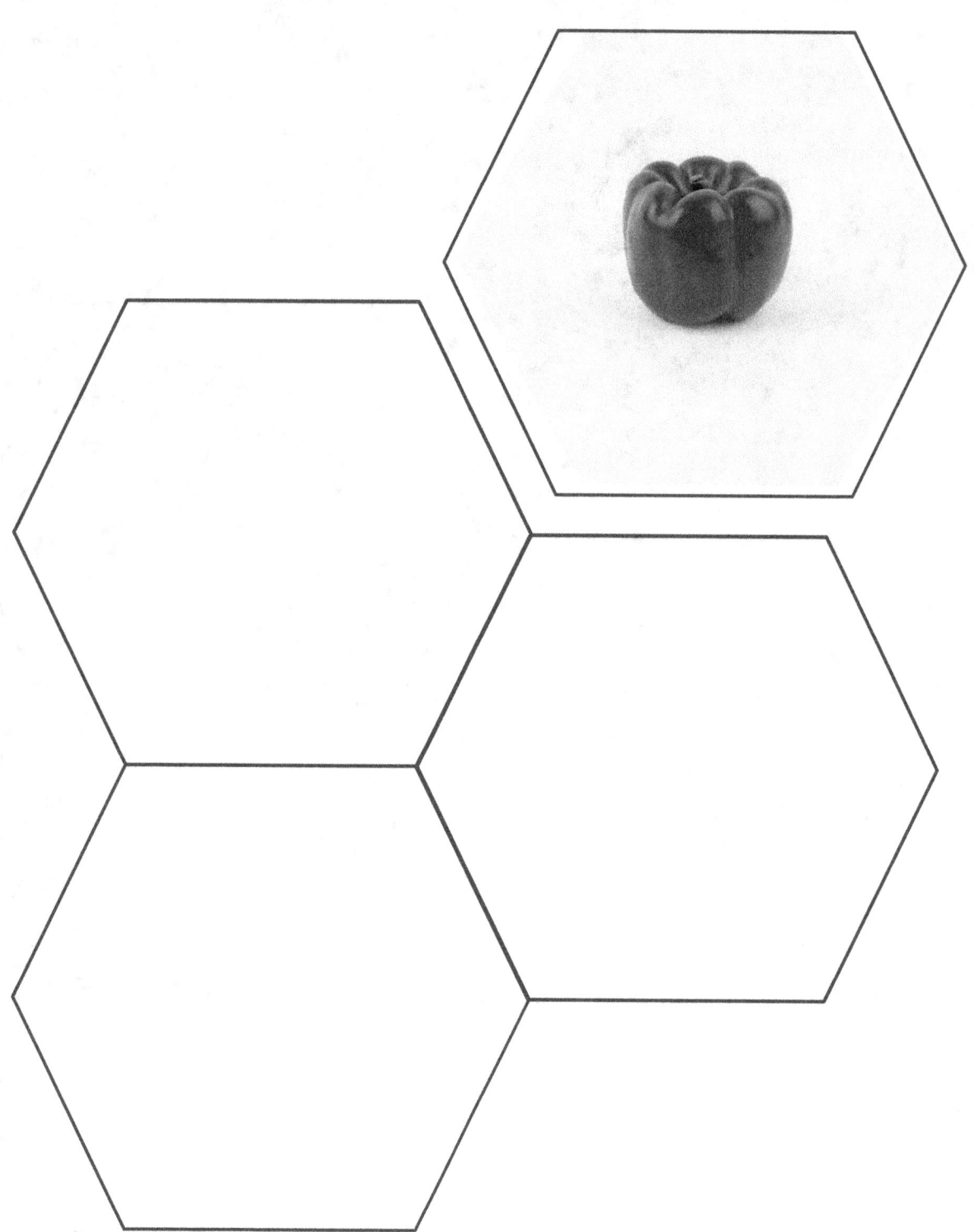

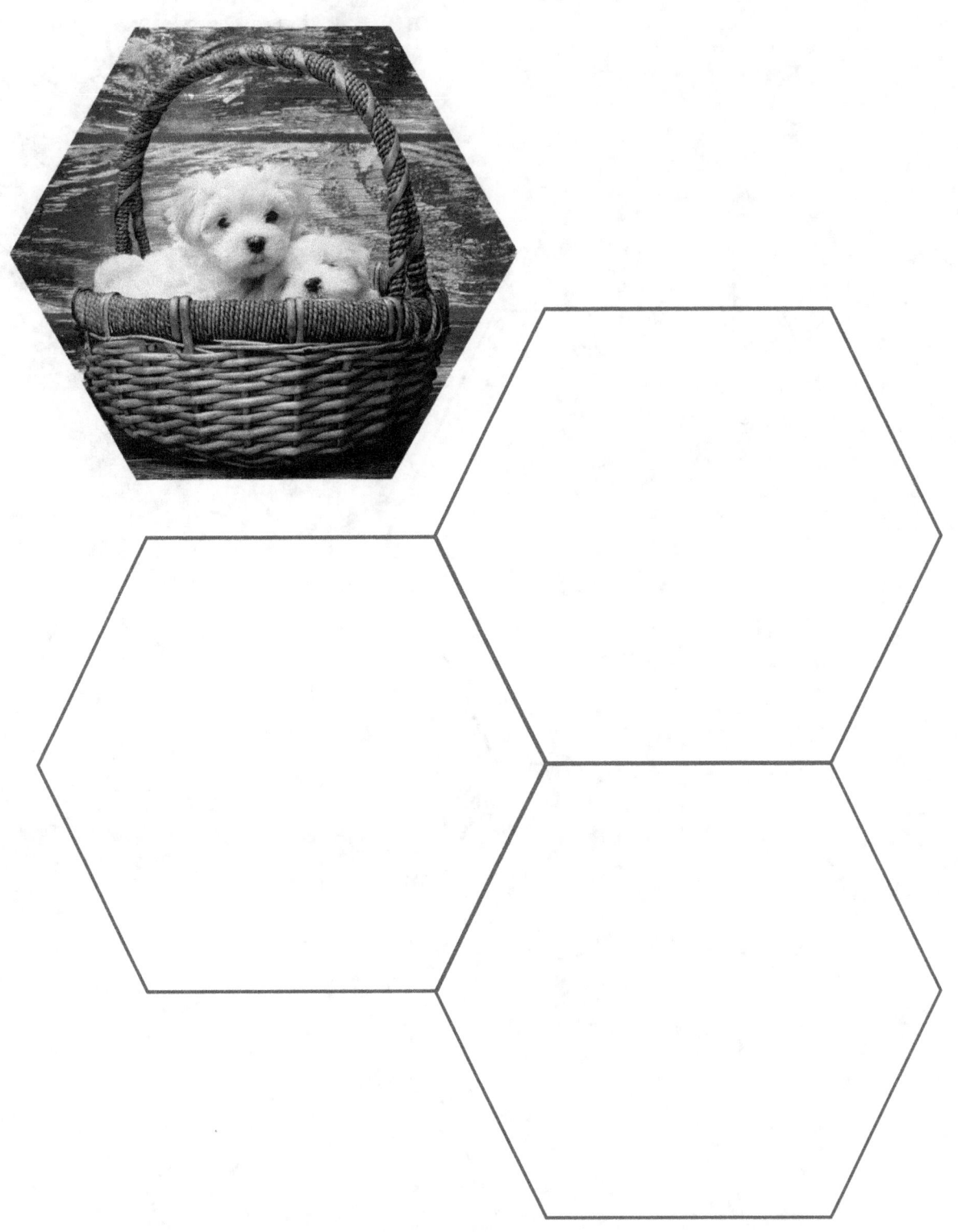

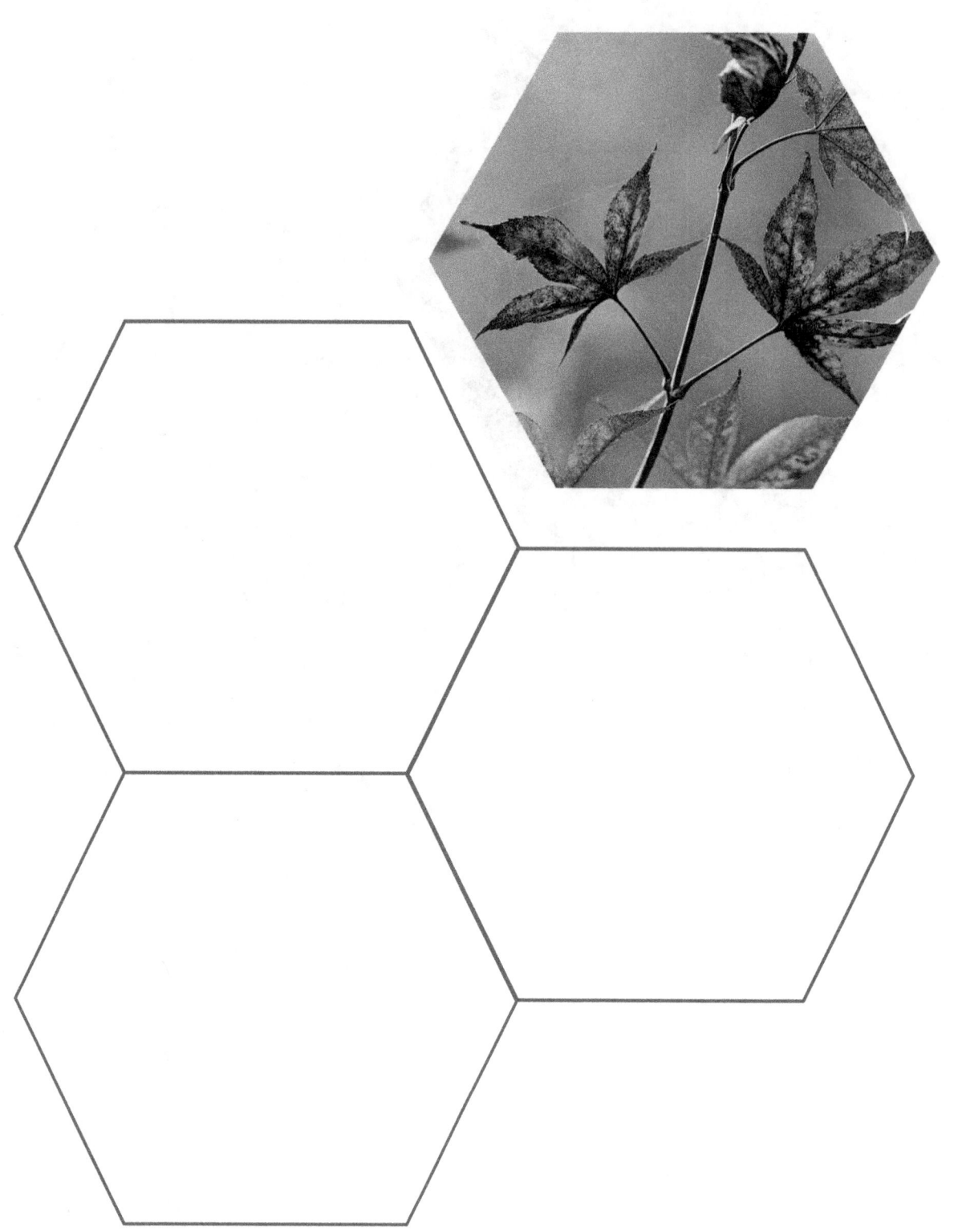

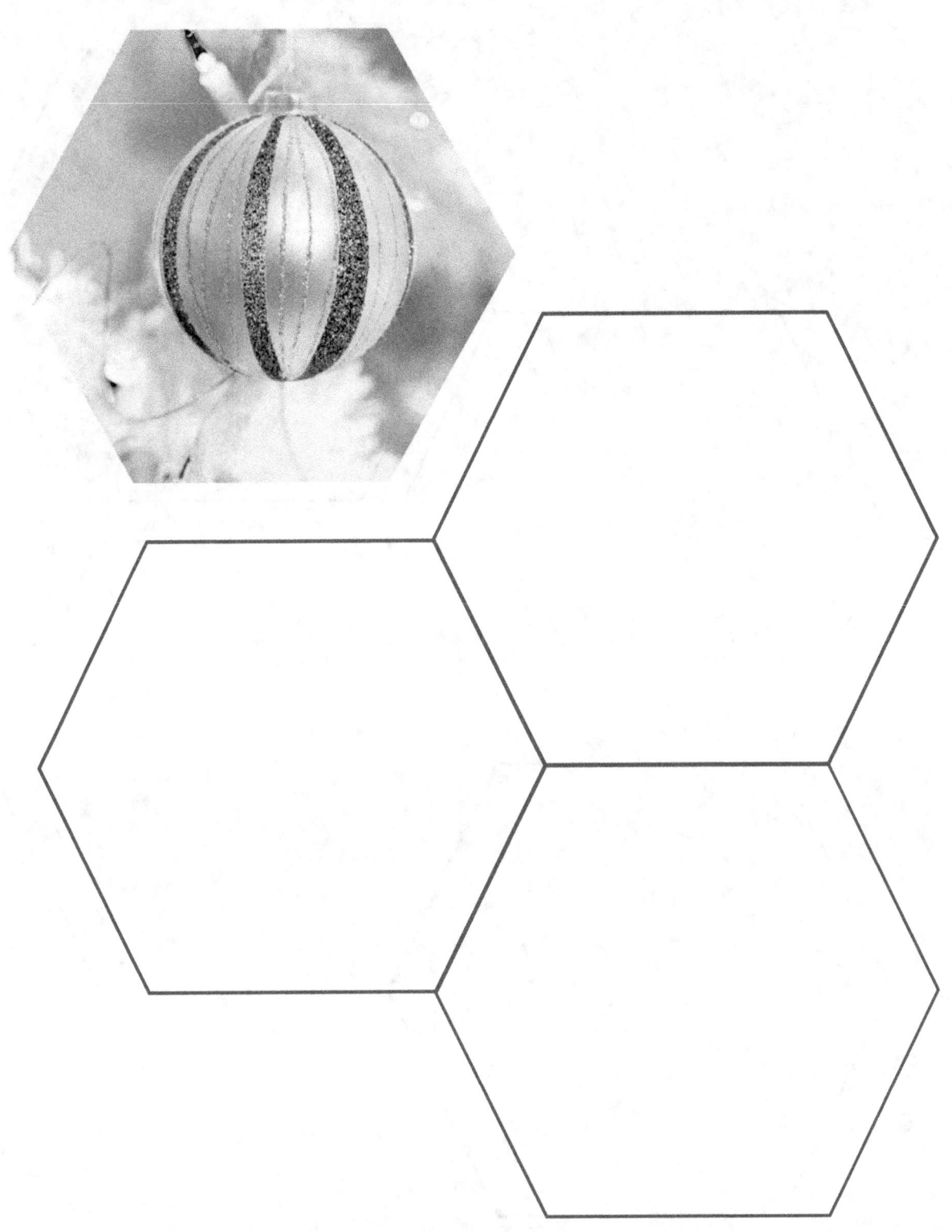

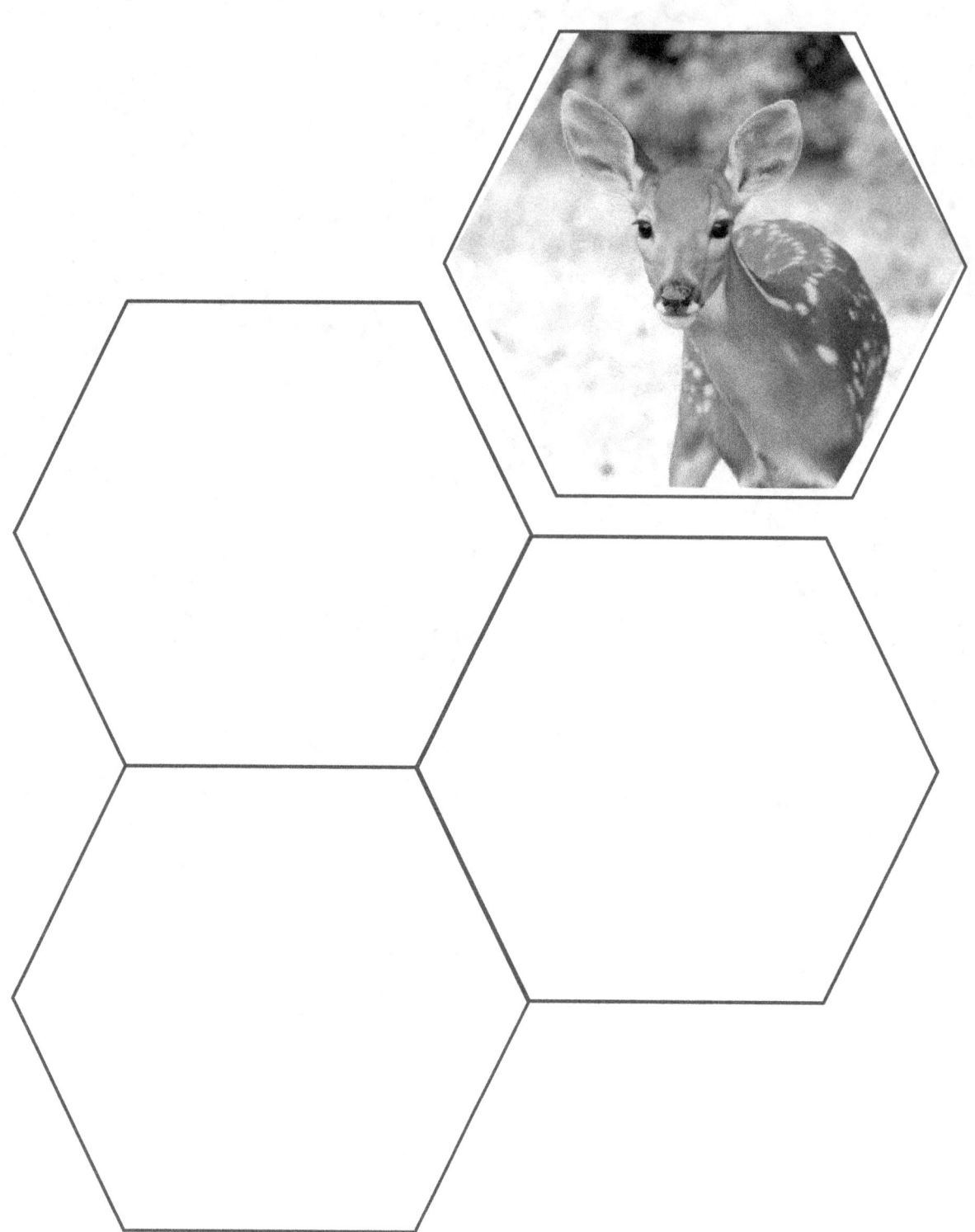

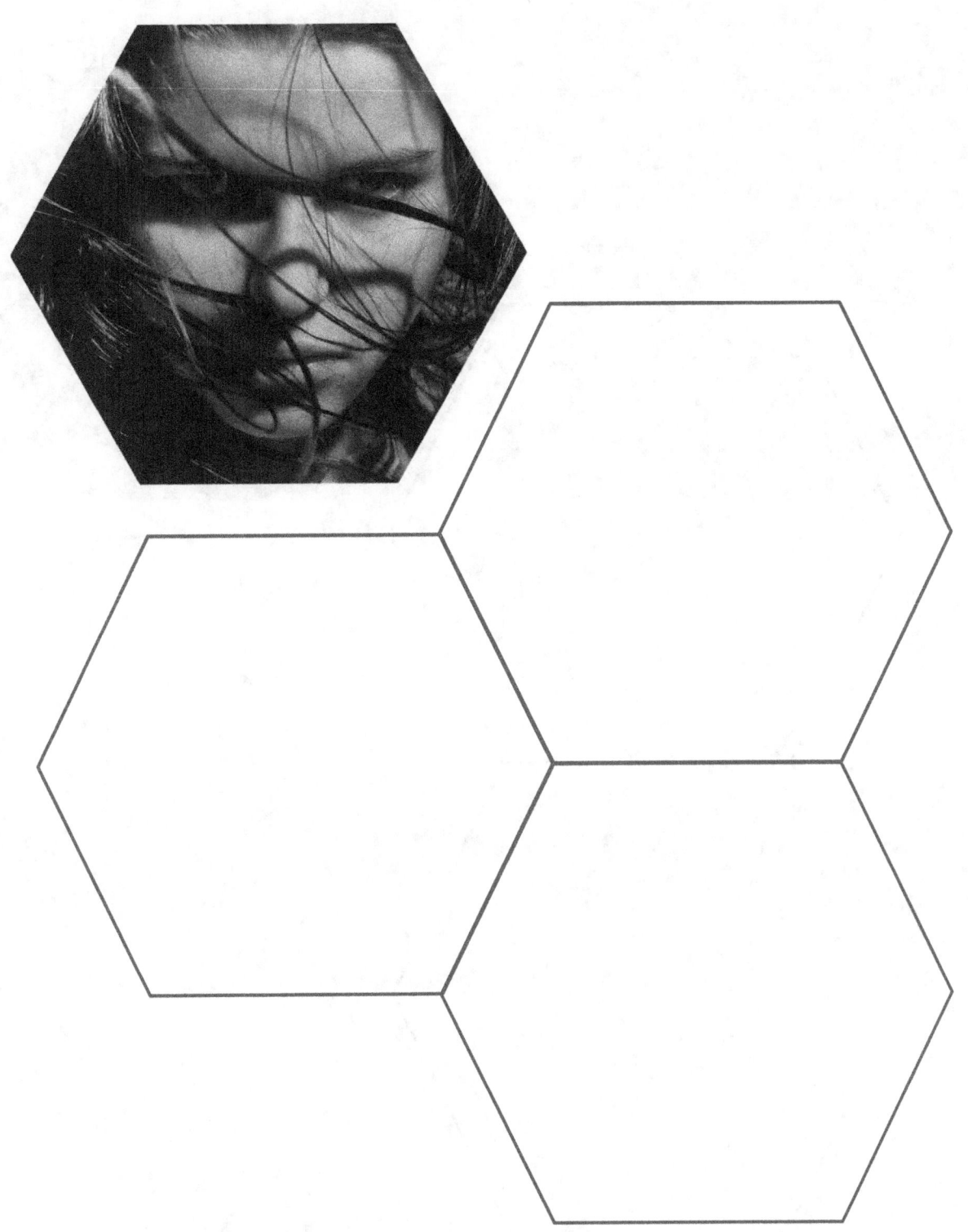

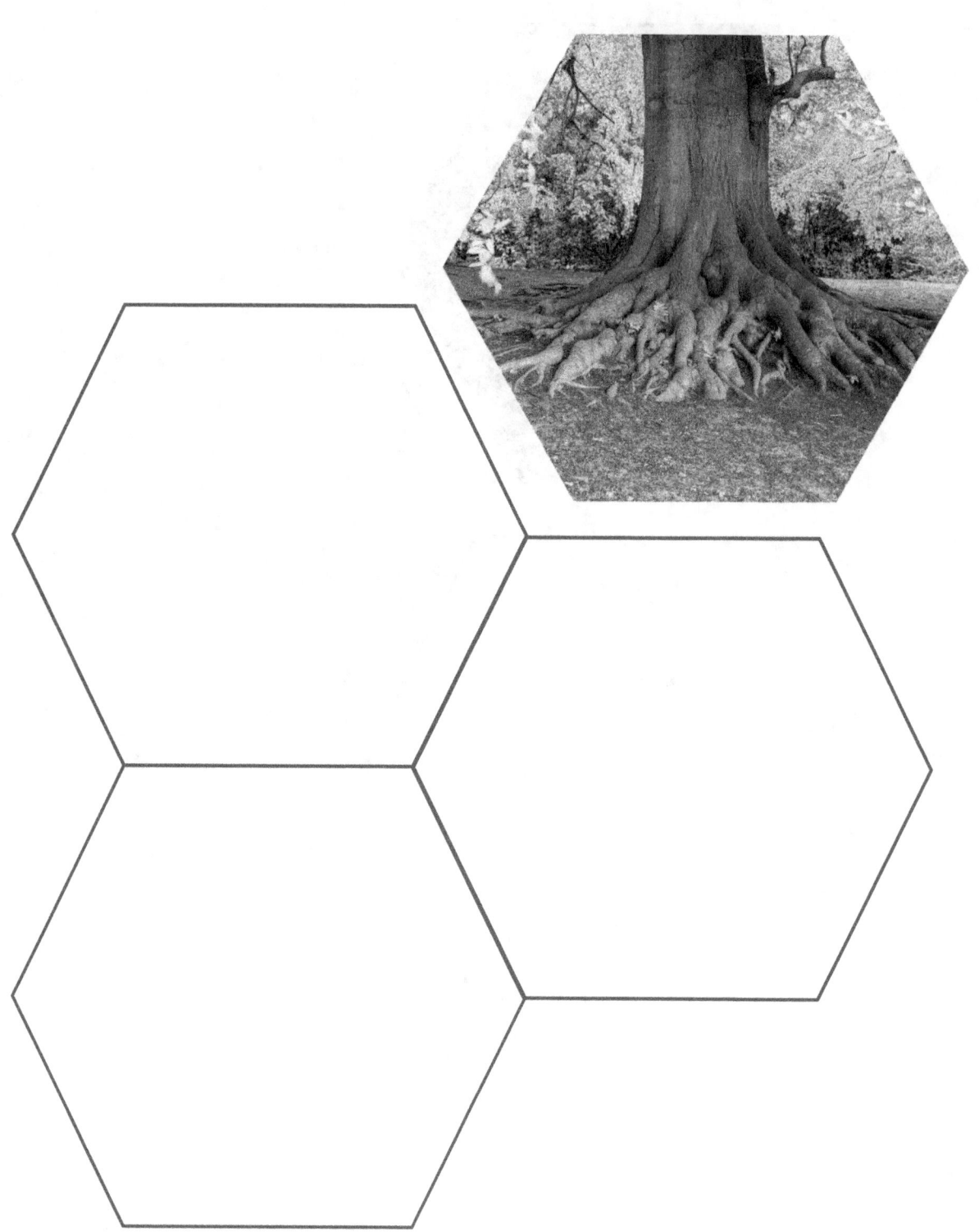

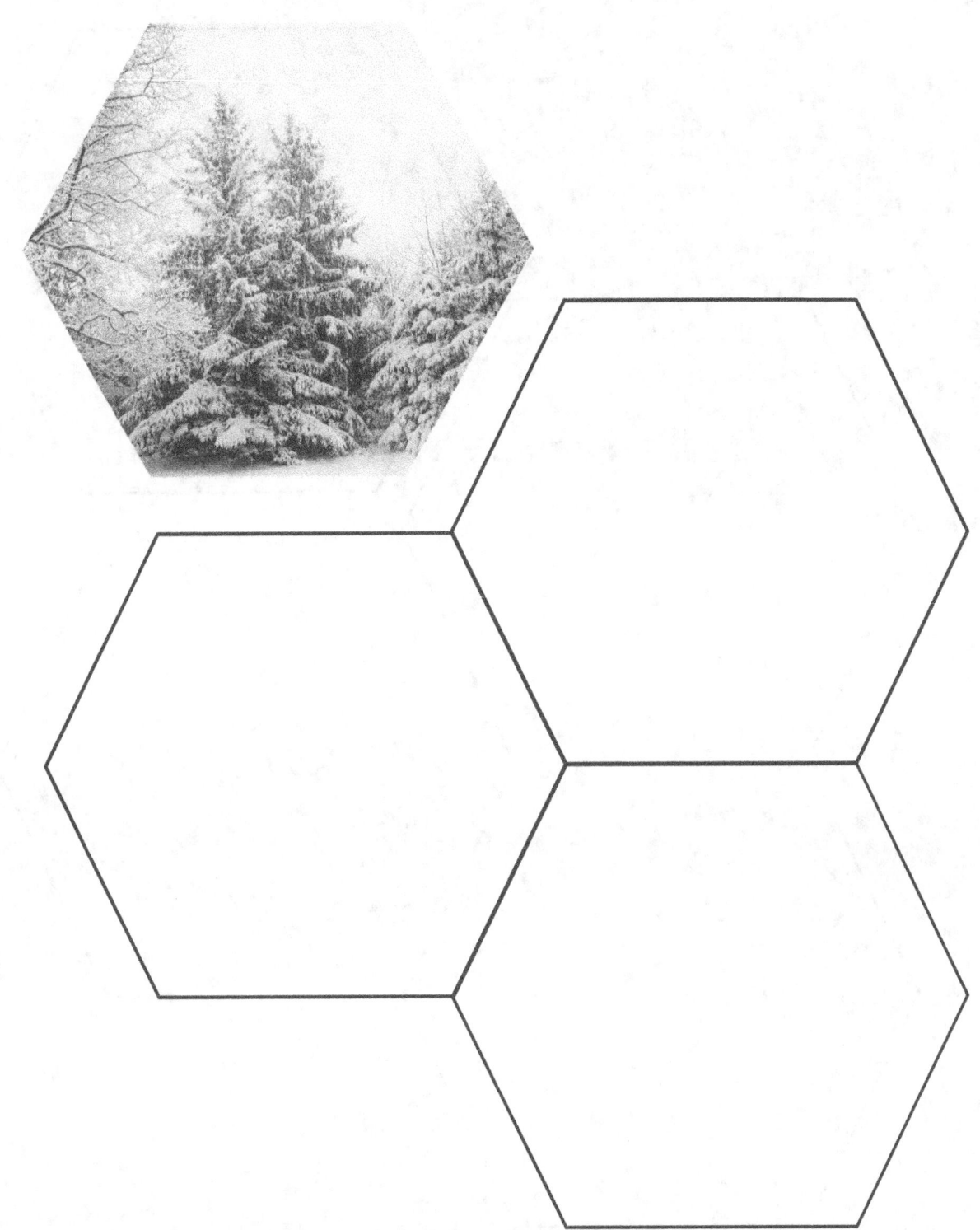

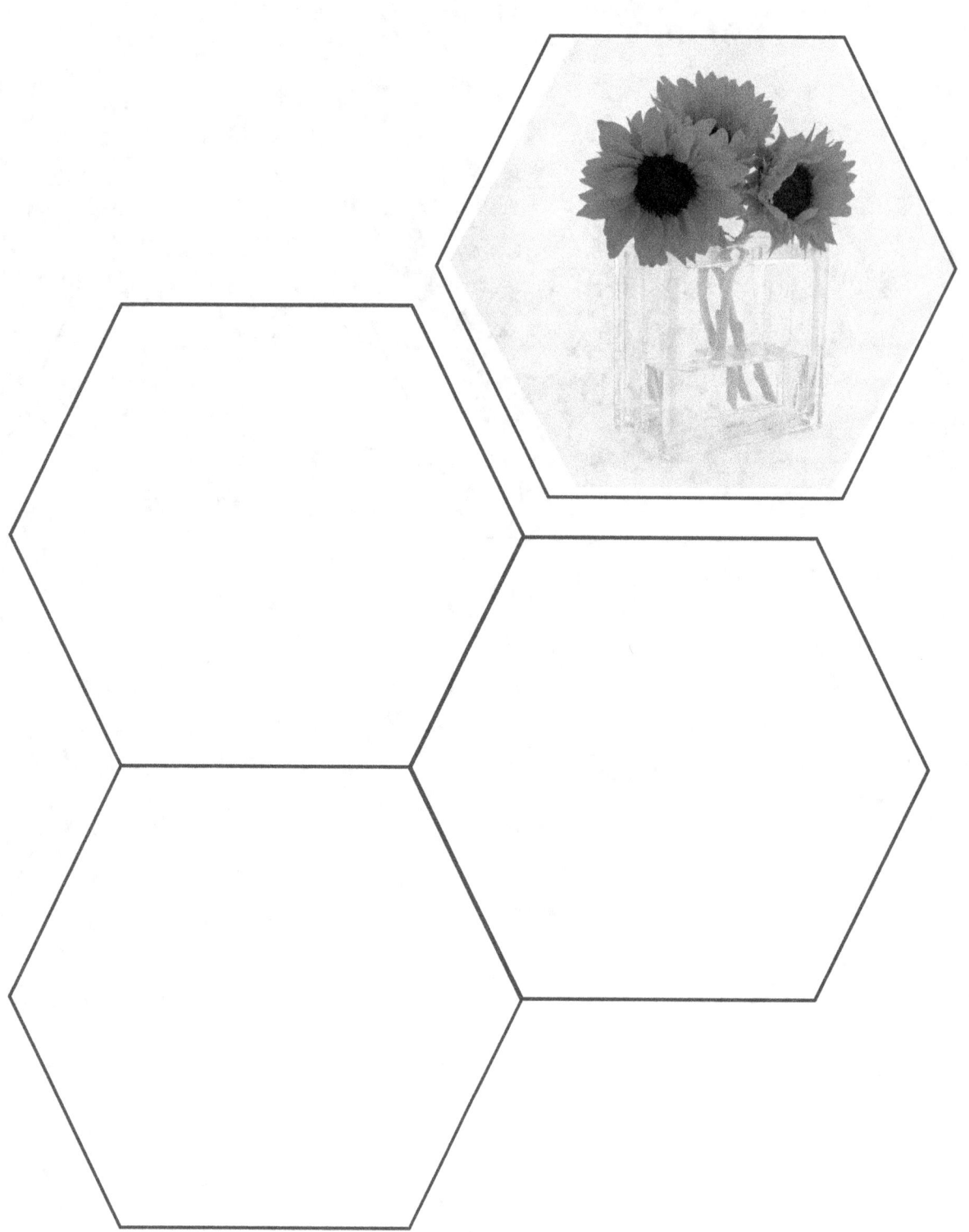

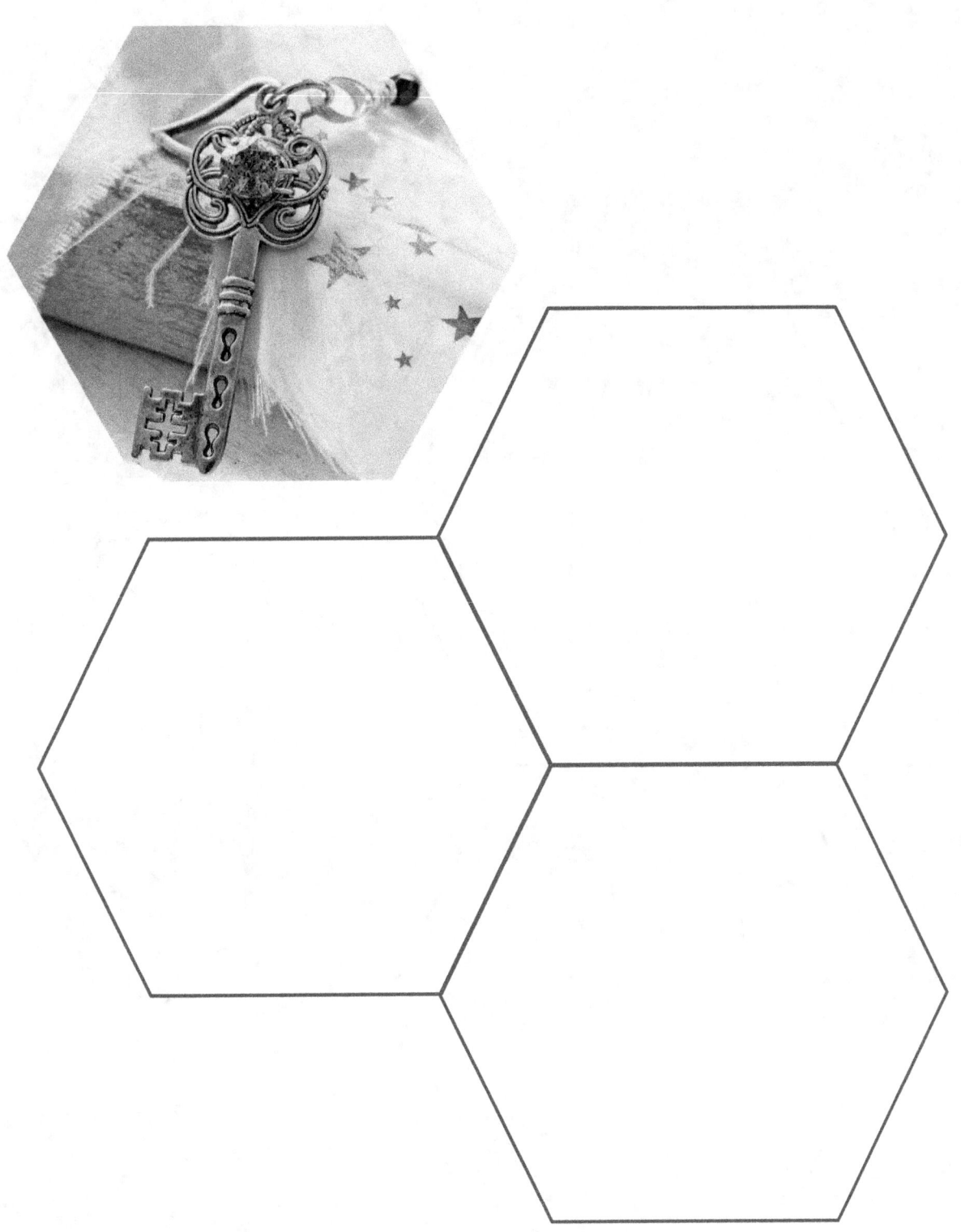

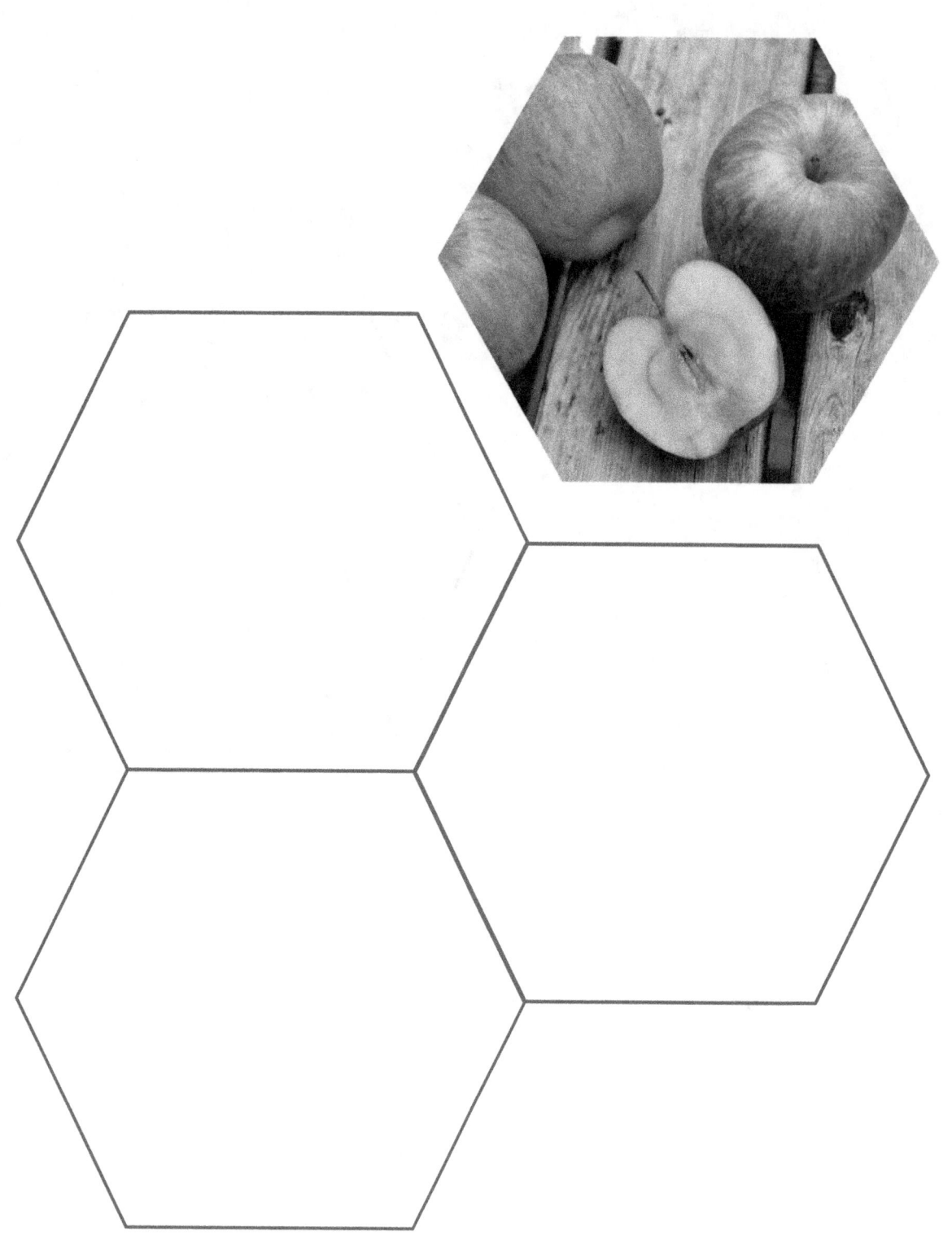

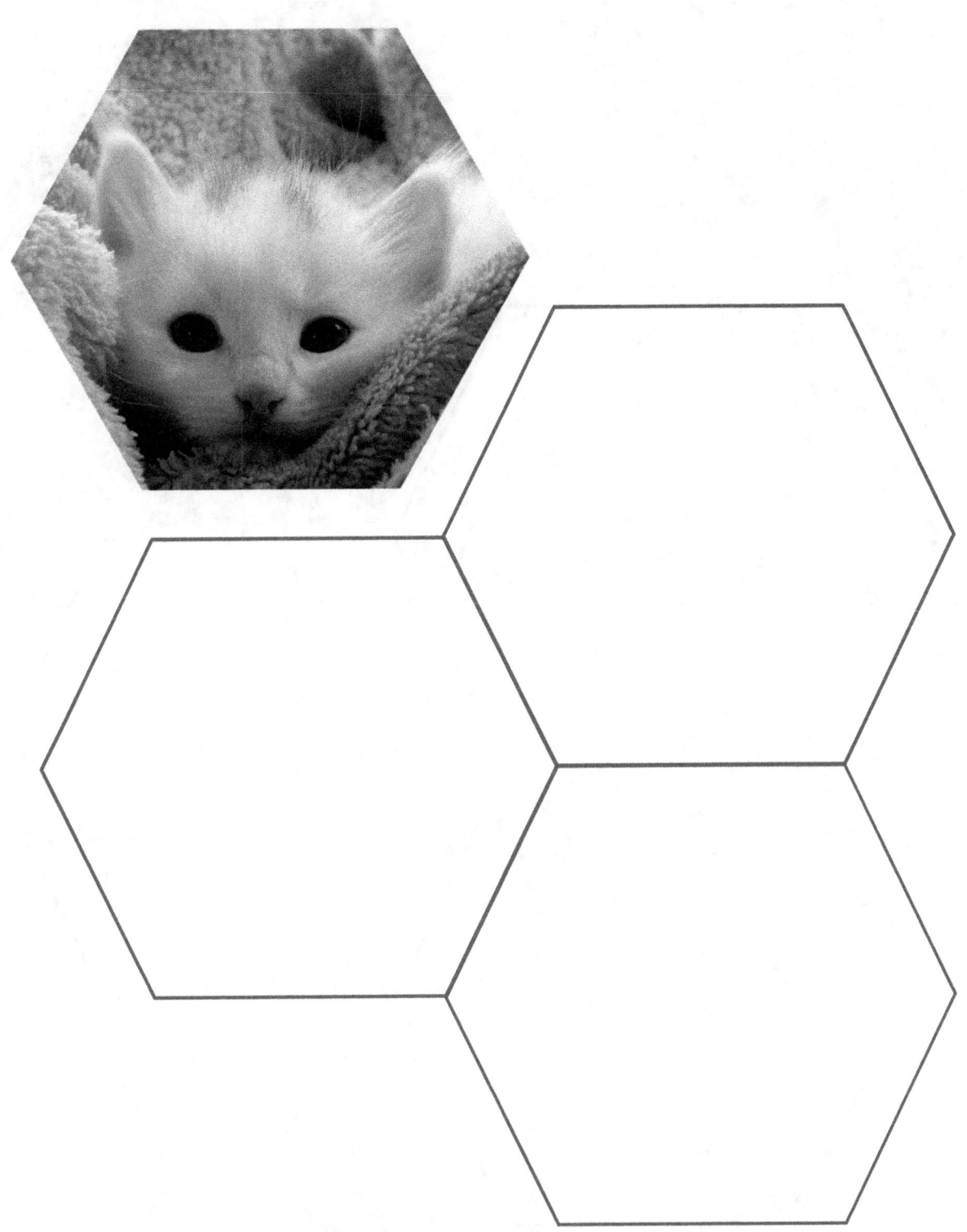

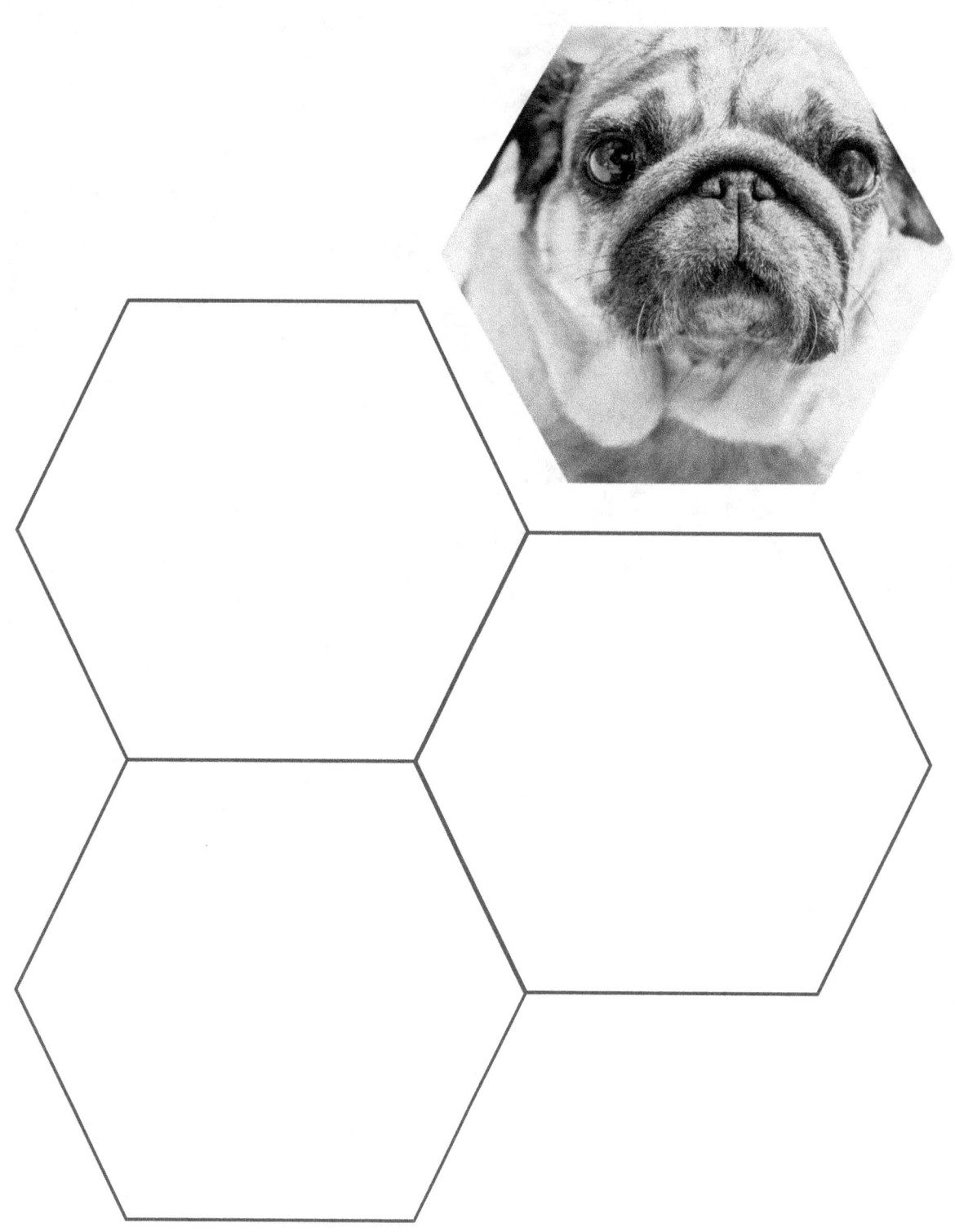

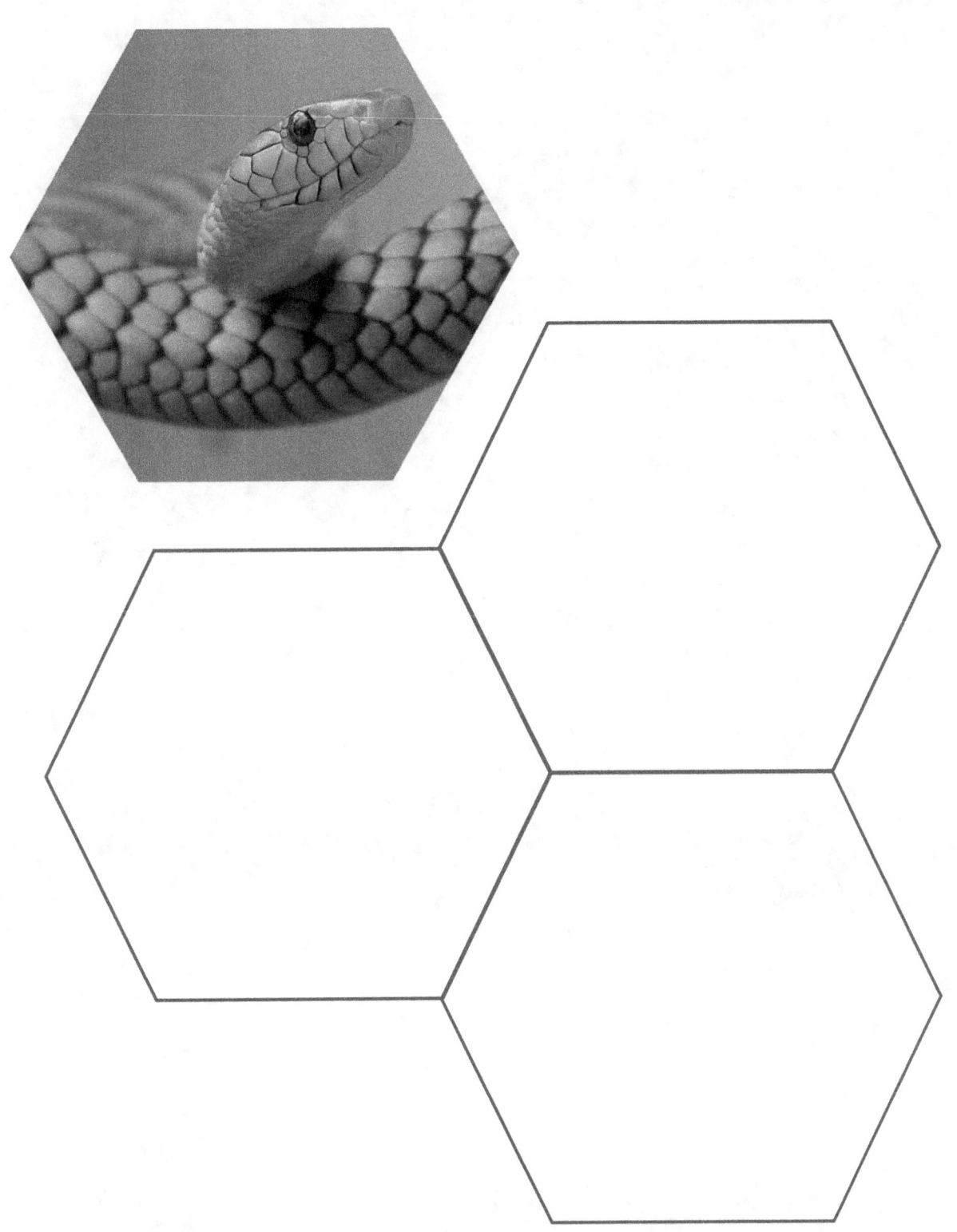

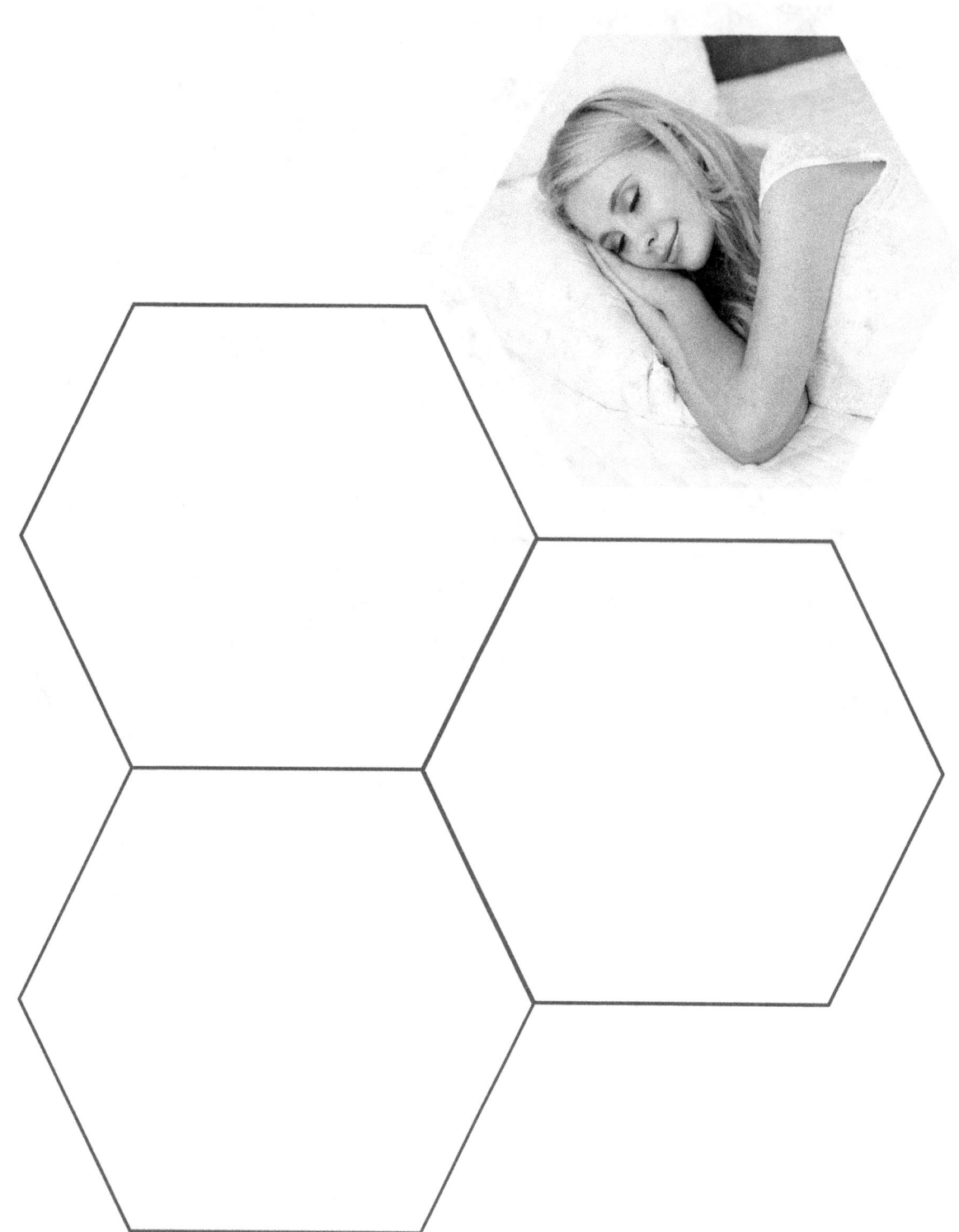

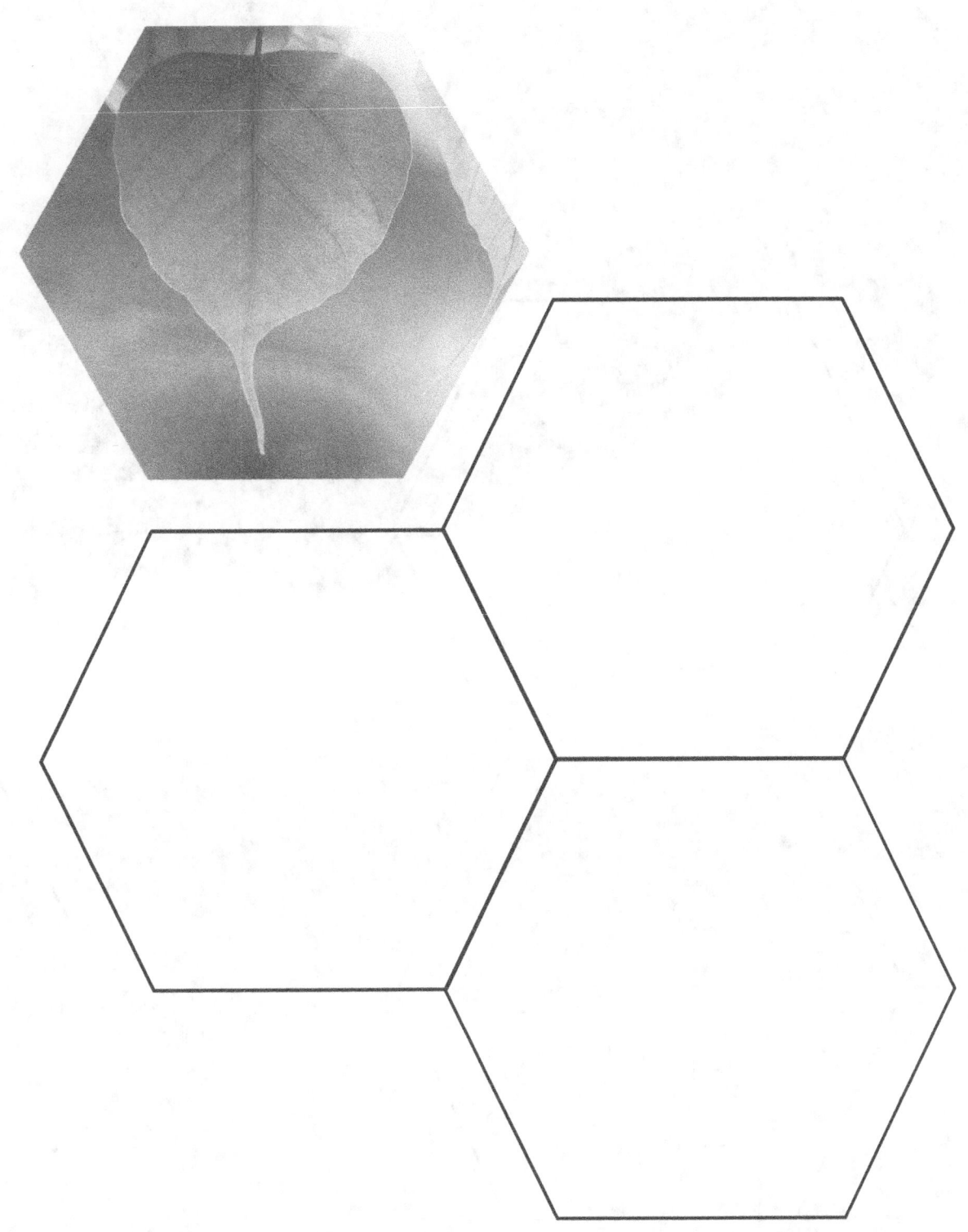

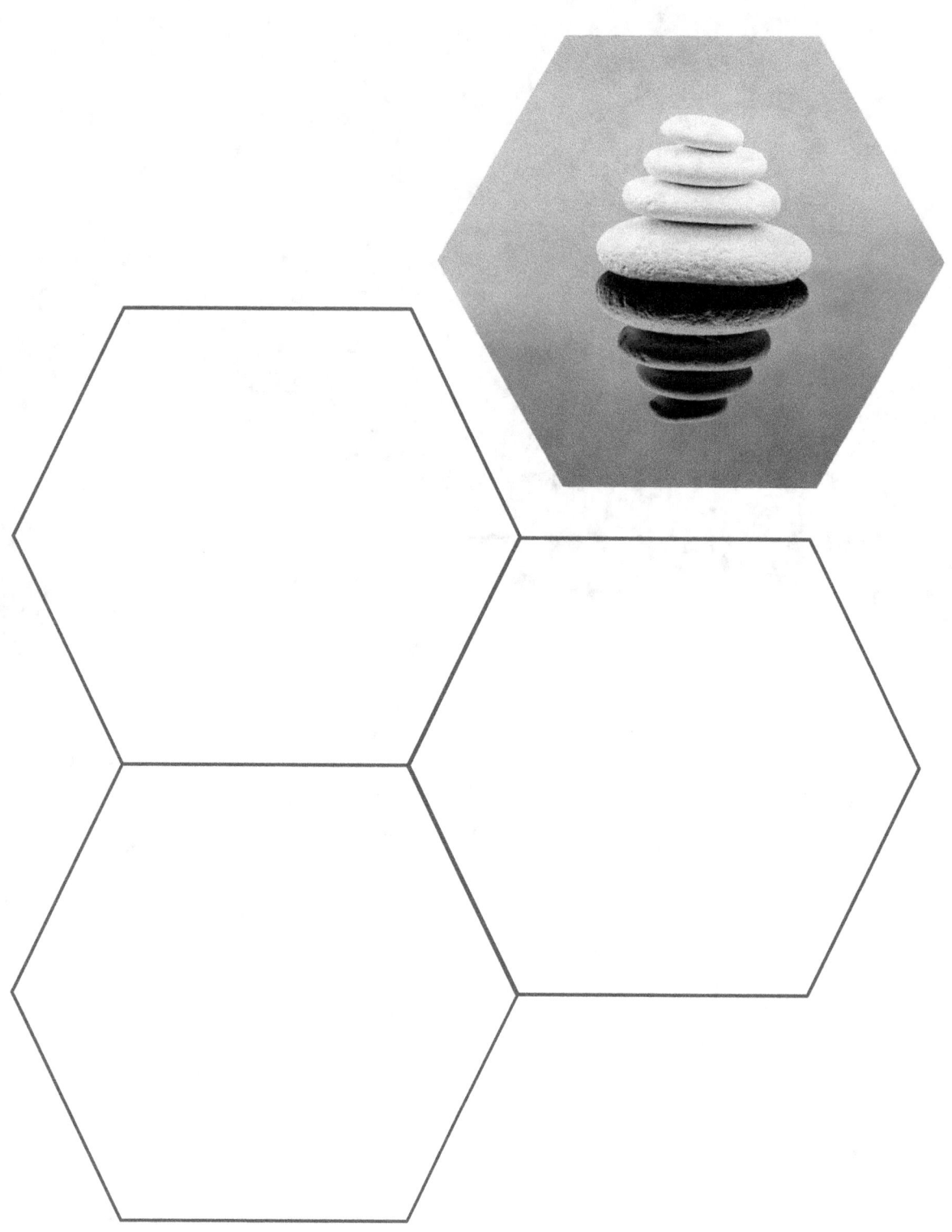

www.ingramcontent.com/pod-product-compliance
Lightning Source LLC
Chambersburg PA
CBHW080600220526
45466CB00010B/3203